Pain in Paynesville

Kirk House Publishers

*To my children, who inspire me to
leave the world a better place.*

PAIN IN PAYNESVILLE

My Firsthand Encounters with Terror and the Search for Jacob Wetterling

KRIS A. BERTELSEN, PH.D.

First Printing: August 2024
First Edition

Paperback ISBN: 978-1-959681-36-6
eBook ISBN: 978-1-959681-37-3
Hardcover ISBN: 978-1-959681-38-0
LCCN: 2023923200

Interior and cover design by Ann Aubitz
Author photo courtesy of John Schmelzer
Published by Kirk House Publishers
1250 E 115th Street
Burnsville, MN 55337
kirkhousepublishers.com
612-781-2815

TABLE OF CONTENTS

FOREWORD

Trauma is a word encompassing many different aspects of the human experience. I first met and became friends with Dr. Bertelsen over a connection to be an advocate for the voiceless, and to help others be able to work through past traumatic experiences. He brings such a strong skillset based on his life and professional experiences as an educator, therapist, researcher, program director, and author. Today we continue to do this work as a mission to help others heal from past wounds.

In this book, Dr. Bertelsen presents a gripping first-hand account of the terror boys experienced in a small town. You will gain insight into boys' experiences during a string of rare crimes detailed in this book, and be able to understand more of the context surrounding the Jacob Wetterling case than has been previously depicted.

This is a must read for any true crime enthusiast, childhood trauma victims, or anyone who treats people with childhood trauma.

~Jordan Howard, LPC-S, Ed.S, MSMFT

INTRODUCTION

This is a book I never imagined I'd write. It came about in a dramatic turn of events that were nearly 30 years in the making. The events that took place in my hometown happened in the mid-1980s. At the time, we were focused on protecting ourselves and staying safe. I'm sure none of us ever imagined the crimes Danny Heinrich would go on to commit or the subsequent investigation. By 2013, when things started happening again, I had long given up on there ever being resolution of any kind to the crimes I wrote about in this book. In my mind, I had accepted as fact that we'd never know who the perpetrator was. The level of uncertainty during the events themselves, and the way uncertainty affected me as I grew up after them, were often nearly unbearable. Of course, much of that is described in the book. As you read, I hope you will imagine what it was like for us as we went through these times, and even more importantly, how these experiences—and your own—may be helpful and useful to help others.

I have found in life that some events make no sense in the moment, but in time become clearer. The cases I wrote about affected many people, often for decades, and for many, forever. In my own life, it became clear long before the cases were solved, that I would have to work to heal, or suffer the consequences. In fact, I started my own healing journey from the effects of the Paynesville cases in about 2000. Trauma and its effects were insidious for me as I had gotten so accustomed to feeling hypervigilant. I got to the point where I wanted to feel internal peace in my life, despite my experiences as a young boy, even if things weren't always peaceful on the surface. The work required vulnerability and effort, but the results can be a huge asset to oneself and others, Because of this work, I have been able to be of service to others in some meaningful ways.

Despite people living in the uncertainty of the cases, in the intervening years from when the events took place to when the cases were resolved, many positive things took place. Some of these include increased efforts to educate people about child safety, awareness and attention to crimes against children, and an increase in the ways law enforcement, schools and communities communicate and respond. This is not to mention the personal challenges and resilience shown by people involved in the cases including victims, witnesses, law enforcement, and other professionals.

I felt compelled to write this book because it is such an intriguing story with so many connections. I'm hopeful that I gave a perspective that helps people learn about the backstory and add to their knowledge of the case. Further, I wanted to underscore to the boys who experienced the events in Paynesville that their experiences matter. It's my hope that people see experiences like these and their own make a positive impact in their communities and in the lives of others.

PROLOGUE

*In the depths of winter, I finally learned that within me there
lay an invincible summer.* ~Albert Camus

The off-key tone and vibration of everything near a train
are unmistakable. Train whistles always give me the
chills. The closer to the tracks, the more intense the ca-
cophony. That a train would rumble by the therapist's office
with the whistle blowing in that familiar, haunting, chill-induc-
ing tone was fitting and ironic. Although more than 30 years
older and nearly a thousand miles away from where I grew up,
the train whistle took me home. Its lonely, pleading tone reminded me of the Soo Line Railroad, conjuring up some of the
very memories I had set out to heal with eye movement desensitization and reprocessing (EMDR), in what was intended to be
my last therapy session.

More than one professional therapist has told me if only sta-
tistics mattered, I'd be in prison, submerged in chemical addiction, or dead, a result of finally succumbing. Gratefully and surprisingly, this is not the case, though I have struggled. Some
people, myself included, would say I attempted to kill myself
with the numbing effects of alcohol. Statistically, I certainly
would have been a long shot to finish college, let alone graduate
school. This is not a religious book per se, but other than God, I
don't know any other way to explain what else, if anything spe-
cific, made me dust myself off over the years, persist, and be

resilient while other people suffer so immensely, perpetually. It's troubling and disturbing to watch people struggle, fighting chemical addictions, flailing in unhealthy relationships of all kinds, one after another. That list goes on ad infinitum. I believe God allowed me to use my experiences, make my mistakes in life, and live to tell about them, for a purpose: serving other people. Unequivocally, I'm not writing this book to heal. Friendships and extensive therapy have helped me in the healing process already. Of course, people are the sum of their experiences, their reactions, and influences in their lives. While circumstances affect many aspects of life, fortunately, we do get to choose how we move forward, accept, find purpose, and grow. Writing this book isn't even for me. There's no need to do it for cathartic purposes. I'm writing to tell an unbelievable story, analyze, reflect, and attempt to be helpful to others who are trying to heal or presently going through their own difficulties.

In my hometown, the train tracks ran east to west, and a trestle allowed the train to cross the Crow River right on the northwestern edge of downtown. Winding its way through Paynesville, Minnesota, one particular stretch of the river was a favorite place for us. Adventures to this spot would begin with an offhand comment like, "Hey, I got some smokes; let's go down to the river." We'd be on our way. Working our way down the slope, we would navigate the often slippery, well-worn trail down the embankment right next to the train trestle, our feet sliding on the chunks of ground-up granite rubble used for the track bed. Below the milk plant, we would spend countless hours between the tracks and the river. There we swam when the water was deep enough, built small dams when it wasn't, floated on inner tubes, had bonfires, smoked cigarettes, fished, and camped. A group of us boys, whom I affectionately call 'Misfits,' spent a lot of time together in the mid to late 1980s. Although some people in town may have said it, we weren't what you'd call bad or rotten kids. We just didn't fall into any one social group (clique) and didn't want to. Some of us were in band and sports but still loved to hang out at the river. Still technically in town, yet secluded, this particular location was great because of its proximity to the woods and the river. Varying in composition here and there, about ten or so in number, we Misfits were carefree, daring, adventurous, relatively innocent, and—by today's measure—naïve, which I address later, specifically demonstrating it with a story.

Growing up in the 1980s was markedly different from today for a whole host of reasons; it really marked an upheaval in the way we lived in central Minnesota and beyond. Jacob Wetterling, a kind, happy, innocent boy, was abducted by a stranger while he was riding his bicycle with friends near a convenience store in his hometown of St. Joseph, Minnesota. In a case that went unsolved for decades, his disappearance—the story of his family's subsequent tireless efforts—changed the way people parent and influenced how professionals respond to sex crimes against children, especially boys. Jacob's story rightfully gained national attention; almost nobody could believe something like this could happen. We, the Misfits from Paynesville, located 28 miles from where Jacob lived, weren't shocked, as we had been living through terrifying experiences of our own.

Haunting many of us to this day, affecting so many areas of life, and leaving a dark, chilling legacy in central Minnesota, this story began over 35 years ago, but painful, agonizing questions persisted, remaining unanswered until just a few years ago.

"Where is Jacob? Who did this to him? To us?" I'll share here how multiple violent attempted and actual molestations—through surprise attacks on boys in Paynesville in the mid to late 1980s—relate to two similar crimes in the area. The other two crimes are the kidnapping and sexual assault of 12-year-old Jared Scheierl 18 miles from Paynesville in Cold Spring on January 13, 1989, and the October 22, 1989, kidnapping, sexual assault, and murder of Jacob Wetterling in St. Joseph. These crimes are inseparable. Jacob's killer, Danny Heinrich—the same perpetrator in the other crimes—walked free for nearly 27 years until 2015. Heinrich avoided conviction for the sexual assaults, kidnappings, and murder due to statutes of limitations. Ultimately, with a charge for possessing child pornography, the government arranged a federal plea agreement, and Heinrich confessed to his other crimes. Heinrich then led investigators to Jacob's remains, right outside Paynesville—near the location where he had driven Jacob, sexually assaulted him, and murdered him.

For decades, I have felt and believed that Jacob and I are kindred spirits, but my purpose for this book is not to tell Jacob's story or his family's, but only to underscore the connectedness.

Walking you through some of my personal experiences—including interactions with law enforcement and people involved with the Wetterling investigation—I'll share how these experiences affected my friends' lives, and mine, perhaps inspiring hope. Almost all of the Paynesville victims were my friends; I knew all but one of the boys personally. At the epicenter of the attacks, because of the group of kids targeted, I learned about most of the attacks right when they happened, or in school the following Monday. However, I will try to concentrate on what I know firsthand—that is, the two attacks where I was present—and on my experiences with the subsequent investigations, such as the report I filed to investigators within 48 hours of Jacob's abduction. With any references to Jacob Wetterling, his family, Jared Scheierl, or anyone else, including law enforcement or the investigation of these crimes, I want to provide perspective and memories of my own experiences in Paynesville, along with the connections to Jared Scheierl's assault and to Jacob Wetterling. I'll focus on what I know or have experienced related to the cases.

My hunch is that few people decide to write a book about these types of crimes, this trauma, without thinking deeply about the potential positive and negative ramifications. Writing the book is important for many reasons: It tells an incredible, fascinating story with irony, twists, and turns. It tells a story in which I never would have envisioned the kind of ending where the perpetrator would go to prison. Neither I— nor, likely, any of the Misfits from Paynesville—thought law enforcement would ever look at the cases again, let alone solve them. Years—decades, actually—went by without action on the Paynesville cases. Jared Scheierl did his own research and found more information. He contacted me, and we quickly learned about striking parallels and incredible ironies in our lives.

Fascinating as the story is, this is neither an investigative, chronological report nor a history of the Jacob Wetterling case, nor a book about Jared Scheierl. Those are stories for others to tell. I'll focus on the connections between the Wetterling case, Jared's case, and our experiences in Paynesville.

Since Stearns County released many of the files in September of 2018, thousands of documents have become available.

Piecing it together and poring over documents sounds interesting, but I lived it, experienced it, and survived it. I'll focus on sharing the feelings and effects. I assert that, up until 2013, this case, to most of us involved, was over. This void, for most of us, became a gaping hole where the answers to our questions belonged. We believed no one was interested, or at least that no one was going to solve it. From the time Heinrich began attacking us in 1986 until we found out who he was officially in 2015, and finally saw him sent off to prison, we had no access to documents; yet the memories and questions persisted for decades—almost three decades, in fact. Those memories, recollections, and questions will be the ultimate source for this book. In some sections, I filtered my thoughts through a more objective lens of the newer information law enforcement released in 2018.

I've read many of the files, including tips from law enforcement agencies suggesting suspects, as well as many transcripts of Heinrich's telephone conversations from his time in jail. The sheer volume of tips law enforcement received must have been overwhelming. Even with today's communication and computing technology, the case would be difficult to solve. We know now that undeniably and inextricably, the cases were connected from the very beginning. For almost 30 years, the answers to the Wetterling case were available, like a puzzle waiting to have the final pieces put in place. On October 26, 1989, within 48 hours of Jacob's abduction, I shared a tip with investigators (you'll see the document later in the book). I know the Paynesville piece of the puzzle well. Unfortunately, the answers lay in the Stearns County Sheriff's Department and FBI file drawers, waiting. Without a confession from Heinrich, resolution required DNA.

With Jared Scheierl's efforts and a fresh view from law enforcement, along with the incredible work of the new FBI team, the holistic review of the cases and police reports revealed DNA evidence sufficient to name the suspect.

Many Paynesville boys lived a kind of hell while Heinrich stalked us, zeroing in on our friend group and terrorizing us, but none of us knew who he was. After Jacob's abduction, law enforcement, including the FBI, came to Paynesville to investigate. Those of us involved in Paynesville ultimately mattered to the Scheierl and Wetterling cases. In the subsequent pages, I'll share a story of interconnectedness with one of the most highly publicized, well-known cases in Midwest history, unsolved until 2016. Authorities jailed Heinrich on child pornography charges in 2015, and in a plea agreement, he confessed and revealed where he buried Jacob.

This, of course, is my perspective, but I'm not the only one. There are many of us—boys, now men—who went through, to varying degrees, similar experiences in Paynesville; we went through some of them together. Some of these men refuse to talk about it at all, while others have ongoing personal struggles related to their experiences. I hope this book is, at least in part, their voice. A sparse few primary sources, including news articles, are integrated here and there throughout the book to give you a sense of how things went and who some of the people are—or were—although I have changed some of their names for the sake of anonymity.

There is a plethora of information available that I'll leave you to peruse if you choose to do so. While I am a teacher at heart, this is not school, and I don't want reading this book to feel that way. When I speculate on events, people, motives, and the like, I will try to be clear and maintain balance. Most importantly, this is a story of persistence, friendship, faith, and resilience. There is reason for hope and gratitude as we observe people who help others, who accomplish so much despite their circumstances.

I may be writing this book, but I would probably never choose to read one like it. As you read, it'll make more sense, but I lived through some things I wouldn't wish on anyone. I'm not in a position to try to compete with anyone's personal experiences, as I know everything is relative, but my experiences affected every area of life, including personal relationships and the entertainment I now partake in. My choices in movies, for example, are most often comedies. Anything including stalking themes, child molestation, or kidnapping is a nonstarter and out of bounds as possible selections. You're about to learn why. Please know if I had my way, somehow, authorities would have arrested Danny Heinrich in Paynesville in 1987; he would never have assaulted Jared Scheierl, and Jacob Wetterling would be alive today. In reality, and so sadly, the course of events took a very different direction. Without a choice in the timing or the ending, I attempt to shine some light into darkness and at least offer insight into what it was like for us. At the very least, I hope you finish the book with an understanding of and a feel for the Paynesville events, the experiences, some clarity, and a few questions. Most of all, I hope you develop a desire to be helpful in ending abuse of all kinds. And so . . .

PART I
DEVELOPING GRIT

CHAPTER 1
Talking About Trauma

A wonderful fact to reflect upon, that every human creature is constituted to be that profound and mystery to every other. ~Charles Dickens

Background

Despite even the most extraordinary efforts, increased awareness, talk, a myriad of government and nongovernment agencies, nonprofits, and advocacy, many children face and experience trauma in innumerable forms. I've heard some of the most unbelievable stories about how people grew up, some in unspeakable, astonishing, even deplorable circumstances. Of course, I would like to see a reduction of pain and trauma for children, known as adverse childhood experiences (ACEs). The Paynesville attacks I mentioned in the prologue affected me and the other boys profoundly. I want to use this section to give voice, empathy, and hope to others who have experienced crime, abuse, or other trauma. Part of my purpose is to give people, boys and men in particular, permission and encouragement to tell their stories. Research studies abound on the effects of trauma on people's lives, but sharing firsthand makes it more real, in my view.

For those who can empathize—not all people can—it's easy to see the experiences we have had, and other abuse situations can cause painful, lasting memories on all sides. Overcoming involves feelings of shame, and addressing the violation victims experience is imperative to healing. Victims experience a wide range of feelings and respond in many ways, including anger and addiction, passivity and compliance, or any number of other combinations, sometimes in an ebb and flow of all of these and more. Caregivers may feel they failed to protect the victim and subsequently experience shame and regret; trapped in those feelings from the past, some are unable to move on. On the other hand, stubborn denial can prevent caregivers from acknowledging a role at all, causing the victim to question their own sanity and their part in the situation. For the perpetrators too, if they realize or know they did something harmful and hurtful, feelings of guilt and remorse must be overwhelming. Of course, there are those with mental illnesses, such as antisocial personality disorder or narcissism, who may be unlikely to feel remorse.

Through years of working and processing, I have learned there are good and bad characteristics in all people. I have learned to separate the good and acknowledge that some characteristics are not so good. Experiences are similar. This process of seeing and acknowledging the good and bad, although circular at times, has been a pathway to forgiveness, acceptance, and peace. Acknowledging what happened while trying to focus on growth and improving myself has been an important part of my life. During the time of the Paynesville attacks, there may have been people and resources available for us, but it definitely did not *feel* that way.

It's time to open the conversations. Having shared stories or tidbits from my past—albeit awkwardly at times, and in impromptu conversations—my experience is that people connect to stories, even stories like this one. Paradoxically, where I perceived vulnerability and the potential for the greatest weakness, and, in fact, expected to feel weak, I frequently found incredible strength. People often respect and relate to vulnerability, taking down walls and sharing of themselves. Depending on where people are in their own processing and work, empathy, followed by deep trust, often develops quickly when a person can say, "Oh, I had a similar experience; I'd like to tell you about it." For those victims who have not processed their painful experiences, things seem to come more slowly, and sometimes not at all. It took years for me to become willing—let alone able—to talk about our experiences in Paynesville. I spent time in bewilderment about what we had experienced. It's a process and journey, but it is possible to heal, accept, forgive, be helpful to others, and to set an example of hope.

Powerful and fear-inducing, shame and denial often prevent people from sharing their stories. Even worse, shame often prevents people from seeking the help from which they would likely benefit greatly. I've been there. Feeling desperate, afraid, and isolated, many people turn to chemicals or destructive processes and behaviors as they seek relief from their untold stories. Like the release of a pressure valve, relief sometimes comes but is often temporary, frequently coming at a high price, such as difficulties or even the ruin of relationships. If cigarettes and snuff took the edge off for me at a young age, alcohol was magical—albeit temporary, fleeting, and false. After the effects of alcohol wore off, I found myself in the same emotional place as before, and most often, worse off than ever.

Gratefully, working through many issues, including the Paynesville experiences, brought peace. Acknowledging and accepting that people generally do the best they can with what they have has helped me move forward. In the past, holding resentments only served to keep me unhappy and unhealthy, with zero effect on the people or institutions I resented. Realizing this affected me profoundly because it gave me power back—the power to choose. I'll spend more time on healing and ridding myself of anger and resentment later, but the fact is that trauma, crime victimization, family secrets, and family systems in which secrets are the norm or required come with a tremendous burden of fear, denial, anger, and guilt when the truth comes out—if it ever does. Not to sound clichéd, but the truth ultimately set me free, even though it took many years and much hard work. It was not until I was able to acknowledge and accept all that had happened in my life and work on it, and in some cases, through it, that I was able to be *okay* in my own skin. I think it will be helpful for readers to have some background in the community and the time, and to keep in mind that this story has been part of our lived experience for nearly 40 years.

CHAPTER 2
Paynesville

Now, every time I witness a strong person, I want to know: What darkness did you conquer in your story? Mountains do not rise without earthquakes. ~Katherine Mackenett

This story—and ultimately, Jacob Wetterling's abduction story—began in Paynesville, MN, about 30 miles west of St. Cloud in central Minnesota. I'll use the following sections to set the scene in Paynesville in the mid-1980s, providing the backdrop for the terror that was to come. The background and descriptions will provide context. My parents and I had lived south of Paynesville until I was five years old. My parents then divorced, and my dad transferred to Paynesville, taking a job with the same company. He didn't want to live in the same town as my mom, so Paynesville offered an opportunity for a proverbial fresh start. He rented a one-bedroom place at the Plaza Apartments downtown.

Although I didn't know it at the time, a perpetrator also lived in the Plaza Apartments. This will matter later, but the building and its location are important to the story. It's difficult to be *Minnesota Nice* while describing the Plaza Apartments. Not aesthetically pleasing, to me they were dark, gloomy, and ominous. It was a three-story brick building on the street corner.

I remember the hallways were dark, long, carpeted corridors, dank. Light streamed in from the east end until noon through dust particles where the steel exterior door had a small window. It was dark and dimly lit, with exposed ductwork and breaker boxes in the hallway; if you didn't know where you were, you could easily believe you were in the bowels of a skyscraper or a submarine. The apartments themselves were plain, small, and, with my dad's stuff, cramped. Tucked in the back corner of the bedroom, the bathroom was tiny: a shower, sink, and toilet fought for the limited square footage in the apartment, the design suggesting that the builders realized they needed to squeeze a bathroom into each unit since it wasn't in the original building plans. I can imagine the quizzical looks on their faces when one of them asked, "Hey guys, where is the bathroom?"

There was not enough room for a large kitchen table. With two chairs and the table wings folded down, there still wasn't much room in the kitchen. The one redeeming quality of the Plaza Building was the heavy-duty metal exterior staircase at the back of the building—the type of stairs that vibrated and bellowed like an out-of-tune timpani in a low tone as you made your way on them. You could jump up and down just a little bit, making them vibrate, bellow, and echo. The best part for kids my age at the time was the landings at each floor, especially the second floor. This spot allowed access to a small area, still outside, where it was fun to crawl under the steps and sit. This was a favorite place to play with a friend of mine who lived across the hall from my dad. Jen was one of the two first friends I met in Paynesville, and we have stayed friends all these years later. I'll share more about the other boy, Matt, later. We were all eventually classmates, graduating from high school together.

Jen lived in the Plaza Apartments while her parents' new house was under construction. We would pretend to be on a ship, checking machinery like generators and boilers; we'd climb around the metal staircase or the secret landing, sometimes banging the metal for sound effects. She and I played together a lot on the weekends I was with my dad. I didn't live with my dad full time yet at that time but was in Paynesville every other weekend with him.

My dad was a professional musician for most of his life. Whenever I was with him during his parenting time, every other weekend, he would often play at a dance, typically on a Saturday afternoon or night. Most notably, increases in DWI/DUI enforcement in the 1970s and '80s, more DJ services, changes in overall entertainment options, and the relative costs of hiring live bands versus DJ services made playing in bands every night of the week impossible. However, my dad was able to play on the weekends, supplementing his income. These gigs would generally be for a wedding, anniversary, or birthday party. Back then, at least in the upper Midwest, one could find an American Legion, VFW, Eagles, Knights of Columbus Hall, bar, or dance-hall on nearly every other street corner where people went for live music. Not being old enough to stay at the apartment alone, I had to accompany him. As his roadie, I could be found helping carry band equipment and setting up his drums. The experiences I had in dancehalls, bars, and nightclubs were generally positive. Sometimes it felt good to walk into a place underage and say, "I'm with the band." There were plenty of times when I met kids my age, and we had fun playing pool, walking around, talking, and so forth, even though I would have preferred to be fishing or engaging in other activities, things my dad used to do with me. When I was nine, I moved to live with my dad in Paynesville, and I started fourth grade there. After I moved in with my dad, he transitioned from the one-bedroom unit at the Plaza Apartments to a two-bedroom unit at the Black Saucer, which I'll describe later.

Middle School on Steroids

Reflecting on one's own middle school experiences, most would agree it is arduous for children generally and downright terrible for many. Young people must deal with the social structure in school—including clothes, sports, hair, friends, bullies, fights, drama with friends, hormones, relationships, responsibilities at home, oh, and academics, which include standardized testing. Middle school was stressful for me too, and I tried to get by but never felt like I was a good fit anywhere. This was likely a function of a rough home situation with limited supervision, accompanied by being a child from a divorced couple, which, back then, was not as common as it is today.

The middle school years were the start of some of the most difficult times in life for several of my friends and me. Nevertheless, things actually got worse before getting better. In middle school, I had begun to hang around with kids my dad thought were the "wrong crowd," as he called us. I prefer "Misfits." Maybe he was right in saying that, but I was comfortable with most anyone. It had always been easy for me to relate to people—talking to anyone up and down the social ladder is still easy for me. I was still involved in school activities, like football, hockey, and baseball, but I did other things, too, like hanging around by the river. Unfortunately, like many kids, I didn't make

the best decisions all the time. I learned later that this is consistent with brain development for that age. One major difference in my middle school experience than most other people is
the terror my friends and I lived in beginning in 1986.

PART II
ONE OF THE RAREST
CRIMES

CHAPTER 3
Chester the Molester

One Need Not Be a Chamber — to Be Haunted.
~Emily Dickinson

His face pale, with fear and disbelief emblazoned on his countenance, I will never forget when one of Chester's victims, whom I'll call Adam, recounted his story to me in November 1986. It was not so much the details of the attack I found so troubling and disturbing, even though the details were horrible. All the details of every attack were horrible, in my opinion. There had already been two by this time, if I remember correctly. In this attack, however, Chester cut a lock of Adam's hair with a pocketknife. What struck me so deeply was the look on Adam's face as he said, "The molester got me." He shared his story with me. He gave me the details of the surprise attack, and how he felt. In the expression and tone of his quivering, angry, shaky voice, I could feel his deep sense of loss and violation. As he spoke, I could sense his longing to have his innocence back and his desire for revenge simultaneously. Hearing his story made my skin crawl. He has carried this anger, loss, and frustration for years, as we all have on some level.

At the time the attacks in Paynesville began, I doubt we realized the magnitude the experiences would have on our lives. The impacts began early on and continued for decades.

Intervention

We were not always together, but Adam and I would get into trouble sometimes. He was in eighth grade, and I was in seventh. More than likely, we went down to the river or rode bikes around town, and someone saw us—we may have seen the middle school principal at lunch, but I can't remember for sure. Having skipped school, we were caught. My teachers thought they saw mounting evidence that I was making poor choices, hanging out with *bad kids*, addicted to drugs (I wasn't), or doing something else no good, so the school intervened, setting up a parental meeting.

<table>
<tr><td>STUDENT'S NAME</td><td>SEX</td><td>DATE</td><td>TIME</td><td>REFERRED BY:</td></tr>
</table>

STUDENT'S NAME	SEX	DATE 3/24/87	TIME	REFERRED BY:
Kris Bertelsen	X	XXXXX		Various staff

SCHOOL		HOME ROOM NO.	COURSE/GRADE
Paynesville Middle School			7th

OFFENSE

Kris has missed 14 of 44 days so far this quarter. The staff is worried because he has gone so far downhill so fast that he may not be able to catch up. He has ability and a nice personality, but his attributes are going to waste here at school since he misses so much or is tardy so often. Today he went home with ██████ for lunch without permission and without signing out of school.

ACTION TAKEN

One hour after school detention for not signing out of school. Warning slip sent to parent in hopes of support from home for our concerns here at school.

BY: ████████████████████

SIGNATURE (TITLE)   SIGNATURE OF STUDENT

PARENTS' COPY

Discipline referral from Paynesville Middle School 3-24-1987.

The purpose of this meeting was to get to the bottom of why I had slid so badly academically, in attendance (by that time, as you can see in the notice, I had missed about 14 out of 44 days of school), and with behavior. I would often miss school or go numbly through the motions, not doing any work, or joke around, being a class clown, and making people laugh. I had been a decent student and rarely missed school previously, but my grades had become abysmal, and my attendance was infrequent at best. When I was there, I wasn't ever truly *present*. Certainly, the change in me had been swift and dramatic. They wondered what had happened to the good kid they knew, and their motives and intentions had to do with my best interest. I understood what their concerns were, and I was hopeful the last couple of months of school would go quickly so I could get to summer. What the teachers and school officials didn't know was the terror already beginning to sweep through the lives of Paynesville Middle School boys.

I've always found it interesting, in hindsight, that these things happened the way they did. We boys went on with life, more or less, adapting to the fact that a masked attacker might grab and grope us. I have a hard time describing this contrast: going to a football game like any other kid but riding home on a bike on the lookout for a masked man.

Ambushed

Horrific, yet by that time, we almost expected it to happen—predictable, actually, given what had been going on for months. I knew instantly what had happened when I heard my friend, whom I'll call Kirk, scream, "You already got me, you son of a bitch!" Intense terror choked me; my breath stopped. With a flush of adrenaline, I turned right and saw Kirk, stopped in the middle of the street just short of the block of the apartment where I lived with my dad. Only the pounding of the predator's boots—combat boots—on the black tar of the church parking lot matched my heart's pounding. I tried to see him, identify him, and see where he was running. He was fast, not exceedingly tall with a somewhat stocky build, but he could run. Like an outpaced athlete losing a race, I got a sinking feeling knowing I would not be able to catch him—even if I took off running. This wasn't the movies. Besides, I was thirteen. Had catching him even been possible? What was I actually going to do to him anyway? We all knew of him. We had this involuntary, fearful relationship with this unidentified creep. Throughout this book, I will refer to the stalker in Paynesville with interchangeable monikers: "Chester," "The Molester," or "Chester the Molester." We called him any of these. He didn't have a real name to us. He had been accosting, grabbing, groping boys at knifepoint, and taking trophies in my hometown for months by this evening, close to midnight on May 16, 1987. That night changed my life.

Kirk and I were riding our bikes home that night from Papa's Pizza in downtown Paynesville, a town of fewer than 2,500 people in central Minnesota. Papa's, as we called it, was a popular place for teenagers. Most of us hung out at Papa's after movies or sports events. Often packed on weekends, it was a local place with several video games and at least one pinball machine. Video games took up the front part of Papa's, separated from the dining area. As you went in the door, you could walk straight ahead into the dining area or turn left and go into the game room, which was behind the building façade of large glass windows—likely where Chester had seen, and subsequently stalked, us and several of his other victims. Across the street to the east, and up the block to the north from Papa's, the Koronis Cinema was another favorite teenage hangout. Finally, about a block from there was the bowling alley with a roller rink downstairs. Years later, we learned that, at the time he was attacking boys in Paynesville, Chester lived in the Plaza Apartments, where my dad had lived before I moved up with him. As I mentioned, I had been visiting my dad every other weekend for a few years while he lived at the Plaza Apartments.

No doubt a haven from which to watch us young boys, from his apartment, Chester had a bird's-eye view of downtown. He could likely use binoculars to see us kids standing around outside the theater and Papa's Pizza, about two blocks away. Some of the Misfits were nearly always the last to leave downtown at the end of the night, too, often riding bikes home. The Plaza Apartments were only a few blocks from the elementary school, too. Adam lived a block or so from there. Kirk and I lived on the same end of town; my place was first on the route to his. A good friend, and a few years older than me, I felt safe with him. Given the attacks that had been going on for the previous months, there was literally no way I would go anywhere in town alone by that point, but especially not at night. Things had changed. By that time, many boys around my age had already begun focusing on safety in numbers, not being alone after dark. Unbelievably, this did not stop Chester. Astonishingly, he would attack even when there was more than one boy present.

As you'll see throughout the book, this point is of utmost importance. Inconceivable as it seems, he went after boys in groups numerous times—in Paynesville and later elsewhere.

Within a block of my apartment, traveling south, Kirk and I went around the corner, turning right, and began heading west toward my apartment, which was straight ahead. We had planned that Kirk would stop there to make sure I got into my apartment safely, then continue south on Burr Street, cross Highway 4, and ride the last two to three blocks to his place before calling me when he got home. I was on the inside of the block as we rode our bikes south, but as we went around the corner to go west, we switched places, and I ended up on the outside.

One of those late-spring Minnesota nights—not hot and sticky like summer can be, not cold and damp like early spring, but just right—the warm night air smelled like spring with a small dash of summer. I recall feeling good about the warmer weather coming and the fact that school was almost over for the summer. Recall the intervention I described earlier; by that time in my life, I hated school. It wasn't so much that I hated learning, education, the work, or the people there, as that wasn't the case. However, due to traumatic experiences, and what I now know is post-traumatic stress disorder (PTSD), school had become secondary to survival—simply a place I had to go every day (or was supposed to go)—but I was completely distracted with saving myself. I would later grow to appreciate the importance of education and investing in oneself. Not today, though; survival had become my primary obligation.

Several houses on the route from downtown to Kirk's place had blue spruce trees, including the house on the right. These bushy evergreens were ubiquitous in my hometown and in the area generally. As we completed the turn around the corner, with neither curb nor gutter nor sidewalk, Chester exploded out from behind the spruce trees, clotheslining Kirk, stunning us both with a complete, horrible surprise.

He wore completely dark clothes, like paramilitary fatigues; he moved swiftly and stealthily like a ninja—so much so it seemed to me as if he simply *appeared* from behind the trees. "You already got me, you son of a bitch!" Kirk had already gone through this back in February, disgustingly, on Valentine's Day as a matter of fact. Just a few months earlier, Chester had laid in wait for Kirk in the stairwell of the apartment where Kirk lived. Chester wore a mask, and when Kirk entered the stairwell, Chester grabbed him, groped him, threatened him, and took his wallet as a trophy—revolting. The thought of someone attacking another person induces indescribable feelings, even today.

Less than 500 feet from where I lived, straight ahead, I knew this area and street very well. Playing hockey at the rink across the street, going to church, serving Mass, and attending religion classes at St. Louis, this was my triangle, and to my horror, he had now inserted himself into it, planting a flag of terror. I knew Chester was out there somewhere; we all did, but this was an invasion. I went to school with the children who lived in the house whose yard Chester used to carry out his ambush. This was certainly not new in town. As I said, he had already attacked Kirk. How did we not see this coming? Kirk and I were certainly talking and must have taken in a few minutes of peace, enjoying the bike ride and each other's company, somewhat relaxed with our guard down, then wham! One way to describe that night is with a phrase I have heard when referring to a type of military bombing attack called "shock and awe." The negative connotation of the word awe resonates with me in this context. Not awe as in wonder, such as the feeling one might get watching the space shuttle launch or peering over the horizon to see the Grand Canyon for the first time, nor the grand finale of Boston's Independence Day Fireworks (which are incredible). No, this was awe as in stunned, shocked, disbelief that, yes, people can be this terrible to others, and, yes, it just happened to us.

It was such a numbing and mind-blowing experience, and happened so fast, there was little time to react. The moment Kirk screamed at Chester that he had already attacked him, Chester let him go and took off running across the church parking lot. This would turn out to be a defining moment in my life, setting up unspeakable terror. It sank in. I realized Chester was after *me*.

My dad and I lived in the Black Saucer Apartments, an older, drive-in–style motel designed to evoke the kind of drive-in motels you might have seen on Route 66 back in the day. It had a walkway and balcony with metal railings that ran the length of the upper floor. The two-story building was white, roughly L-shaped, with black window trim and yellowish-orange doors on each unit. Walking in, the bathroom sink, typical of a motel, was immediately to the left inside the door, just as you entered the kitchen. The sink was not in the bathroom, but just inside the entry door, right outside the bathroom door. Turning right, you entered the living room. Walking straight ahead, you passed through my dad's bedroom, which was separated from the living room by an alternating striped, black-and-white accordion divider. Running the width of the room, wall to wall, we kept the divider closed most of the time, except for leaving enough room to walk to my bedroom at the back of the apartment. This arrangement meant that I would sometimes have to sneak past my sleeping father, trying not to wake him—either because waking him would mean getting into trouble for something or, later, because he had started working nights and slept during the day. Carpeting covered the entire apartment from wall to wall, even the kitchen and bathroom. In the kitchen and bathroom, the carpet was a deep, late-spring grass-green. I remember laughing cynically at my dad, who, when we first moved in, while admonishing me not to spill anything on the kitchen carpet, was holding a saucepan of tomato soup and did that very thing, thereby christening the floor unceremoniously. The owners, wonderful people, operated the first floor of the Black Saucer as a motel and the second floor as apartments.

When Chester grabbed Kirk—the second attack on him—in plain view of my place, I thought of several scenarios. In a flash, I debated and questioned whether I should go to my apartment, as it would be a dead giveaway of where I lived if Chester were still watching us from afar. The assumption that Chester didn't know where I lived already was probably denial on my part. With what had just happened, I knew he had been after me that night.

Riding my bike as fast as possible to my apartment, I got to the stair landing, dumped my bike, and sprinted up the wooden exterior stairs. My running left the black-painted iron handrails rattling and shaking down to the four bolts into the two-by-fours to which they were fastened because I actually used them, grabbing them to navigate, not wanting to miss the right turn at the top of the stairs. Out of breath, my heart trying to leap from my chest, I rushed into the apartment and called for help. With a 1980s phone cord long enough to be on the phone and still keep watch on Kirk out the kitchen window, I called the police and waited ever so impatiently for someone to answer. In situations like this, time passes so painfully slowly, even though it was probably, at most, a minute or two. At that time, 911 emergency calling was just beginning, and Paynesville didn't have it yet. Making the emergency call now seems ironic because we had a red rotary dial phone. The red phone symbolized the one I'd heard the president had to communicate immediately with the Soviet Union, if need be. The fear of the Soviet Union back then was real, not unlike the fear of Chester, except he was in my neighborhood. It's difficult to imagine these days, but back then, calling the local Paynesville Police number after regular business hours, or when no one answered at the police station, the call transferred over to the Stearns County Dispatcher. I remember it was a woman who answered, and she said she would contact the officer on duty.

My second call was to the Paynesville American Legion, where my dad was playing in a band that night. He said he would send his coworker, who happened to be at the Legion, to help us. After making the calls, I returned to Kirk, still with his bike under the dim, orange streetlight glow. At different times over the years, I have wondered if I *did it right* by leaving to call the police rather than staying with Kirk. Rushing to the apartment to call the cops just happened without my awareness. If I had stayed in the street, I am not sure what would have been different, but I have replayed the scene, questioned my actions, and pondered the question, perhaps out of survivor's guilt. Leaving the apartment to return to Kirk, a million thoughts bounced around in my mind: "Will Chester come back?" "Where did he go?" "Is he still watching us?" Leaving the apartment was a fearful experience, making my blood run cold. Even today, over thirty-five years later, I can feel the feelings return in an instant when I think of it. The best analogy might be a scene of someone frantically trying to unlock a door while the villain is right behind them, or the feeling you get when someone is right behind you and you expect them to grab you. Returning to Kirk, he told me calmly, "I got his hat." We waited there until my dad's coworker arrived. We literally waited right there under the streetlight. We were in the middle of a triangle formed by St. Louis Catholic Church, the hockey rink, and my apartment—a triangle that represented the storm in our lives. My dad's coworker put our bikes in his pickup and took us to the police station. The hat will become more important as the story progresses; make a mental note.

The message to me that "you're next" became strong and evident from the way things went that night. A positive outcome emerged from that evening, too, though. Kirk stood up to Chester, fought back, and barked at him. He had screamed at him, saying, "Chester, you've already gotten me!"

This was an empowering moment for Kirk. He shared that with me, and I'm so glad it was. Getting Chester's hat made us both feel empowered, too, thinking it might be good evidence and lead to the police catching the person somehow. The night marked somewhat of a turning point for us; we both took back some power on some level.

The major takeaway and drawback of that night: he was targeting me—and I didn't know the enemy. Perhaps you can imagine the stress and emotional toll of a masked attacker lurking around the corner in your hometown: behind every tree, in every alley, and behind every partially opened door. We had been living on alert because of the attacks, but this one suddenly became more personal than the others I had heard about. I learned later in life that I was living in a constant state of stress, with stress hormones causing the physical responses I always felt, such as shortness of breath, anxiety, muscle tension, and so forth.

Uncle Bill

Sargent Bill Drager was at the police station when we arrived. We met with him and another officer whom I will call Daniels of the Paynesville Police Department. Drager was a good man who liked kids and was very concerned about the attacks. If no one else smoked cigarettes on the Paynesville Police Force, Bill made up for them, as far as I was concerned. He smoked a lot. The smell was instantly pungent when we walked into the office with the blue air visible, hanging everywhere, wrapping the entire office area as if smoke were part of the decor. I sat worried, wondering, rattled, trembling, and afraid, but Bill insisted everything would be all right. Of course, the experiences in Paynesville had been unnerving and devastating while they were happening. I remember Kirk was calm and collected. He was matter-of-fact and more annoyed with Chester than anything, it seemed to me. I was impressed with his demeanor and change from the fear I saw back in February to power now in May.

In close proximity to me, with a cigarette and smoke billowing seemingly from everywhere into my face, I will always remember Bill Drager saying so sincerely, "If you ever need anything, you just ask Uncle Bill," then admonishing me to be careful and to do whatever I had to in order to get away from Chester if he ever grabbed me. I knew he meant it, and I took his advice literally. Drager worked quickly and hard to enlist public assistance in catching the perpetrator. He went to the Paynesville Press newspaper to bring the attacks to light, with an article appearing in the weekly paper on May 26, 1987.[1] Drager took Kirk's report as he explained what had happened. There are

---

[1] Darlene Thyen, "Local Police Seek Help in Accosting Incidences," *Paynesville Press*, May 26, 1987.

times in subsequent chapters where I will pose questions regarding law enforcement and, frankly, I may sound critical. This will not include Bill Drager. Based on knowing him personally, and how he treated me, it would be unfair to criticize Drager. I truly believe Bill lived to "protect and serve." He had worked tirelessly, in my view, to raise awareness with the public, the school district, and by asking people to help catch Chester by reporting any suspicious activity, and by telling me ways to protect myself.

Stalked

When Chester first attacked Kirk back in February 1987, another officer had taken that report. Now, as we sat in the police station together, I thought how unfair and unreal this was, how unimaginable. Questions raced through my mind: "How did this happen? Why can't they catch him? Does this happen in other places?" Our town was small, and this one person seemed to have the power to destroy all that was good about being a child. Feeling so intruded upon and violated, in hindsight, I must have thought Chester was evil and a coward, sneaking around in the dark, preying on boys who least suspected it. It's more accurate to say I believed his method was cowardly, but it took incredible gumption to do what he was doing, and I was afraid of him. Using these guerrilla tactics, hiding the way he did, ambushing kids, Chester invariably had the upper hand. Imagine your scariest childhood monster, one that could wake you in the middle of the night by coming out from under your bed or your bedroom closet. In our case, he was not imaginary; he was real. He was literally waiting for us, watching for us. It was horrifying. This was small-town America, not the big city.

In other cities, there are neighborhoods bigger than the entire town of Paynesville, and high schools with more people. Yet this unfathomable, rare crime had occurred multiple times. There were at least eight documented attacks—there likely were even more. This is an important point. The rarity and nature of these attacks were part of the Wetterling investigation, which I will discuss later. Although I am not a member of law enforcement, I know that automobile moving violations and kids egging houses were the typical small-town crimes. A masked man, dressed in dark clothing, lurking in wait in a stairwell or sneaking out from behind trees to grope boys at knifepoint, often taking a trophy, is not a common crime—a point I cannot underscore enough.

Rare as crimes like this are, stranger sexual attacks occurred in three different small towns in bucolic central Minnesota, not 30 miles from one another. How did the adults, but especially law enforcement members, not see this connection and put these striking details together? Resolution would be a long time coming but eventually happened. There are a number of moving parts and facets to the story, along with hypotheses about this. This will be a focal point later in the book, but for now, suffice it to say the attacks changed everything for those of us living in Paynesville.

Times were different in the 1980s. We were accustomed to safety, cool summer evenings playing the game *Kick the Can* after dark, being gone from home with friends from dawn until dusk, and camping by the river. We loved the smell of campfire saturating our clothes in the morning. We hung out downtown after the movies or roller-skating, walked through the cemetery as we heard the wind whistle through the pines. We rode bikes wherever we pleased without giving a second thought to going anywhere or doing whatever we wanted, including the roughly five-mile round trip to Van's Beach on Lake Koronis. Kids desire these fun times and memories, not running in terror for one's life from a masked, knife-wielding child molester. What is striking and disturbing to me looking back is how eerily normal it became to live in fear of attack from Chester—a similar desensitization that likely occurs in other tragic situations. It became common to talk about the molester "getting someone," as we called each incident, and people seemed to get used to the possibility.

Based on whom the victims were in the Paynesville attacks, it seemed Chester had acquired an address book and a list of my friends and me—that he was marking us off like a checklist or a notch on a disgusting victim tracking belt. I used to envision a piece of paper—like butcher paper or construction paper—hanging prominently on the wall in Chester's place with all of our names and pictures on a list with checkmarks next to those he *got*. In fact, it was shocking to hear about one attack because it was a friend's cousin visiting from another town, and not one of my inner circle. There was no shortage of amateur sleuthing going on among the kids in Paynesville back then.

Piecing together bits of random information or hearing about sightings or run-ins with Chester over the weekend became common in school on Monday mornings. In hindsight, it seems strange that the big news or gossip from the weekend during that time was not the usual middle and high school talk but something far more serious, nefarious, and grave.

Despite all the talk, even another article in the Paynesville Press[2] a month after Chester came after me, it proved exceptionally difficult—actually, impossible—to catch Chester.

---

[2] Thyen, "Police Still Working for Arrest."

Down by the River

Perhaps we were naïve, or maybe some people would say just stupid, but in the summer of 1988, a group of four friends and I, all 13 or 14 years old, went camping on the Crow River below the AMPI milk plant. I would also point out the underdeveloped prefrontal cortex of 14-year-olds as a contributing factor. This stretch of the river had always been our safe, fun place. I described it briefly in the prologue. Down below the tracks, in town, I thought it had a lot of cool topography, like huge trees that had tipped over, uprooting themselves on one side and leaving nice deep, foxhole-sized places to sit and hide. Twists, turns, and curves of the river bend, along with riffles as well as deeper spots in the water—it truly was our place to escape and have fun.

When the water wasn't too high, we would wade upstream into town and could see the backyards of some of our friends' houses from the water; they'd often come with us. We spent a lot of time down there after school, on weekends, and during holiday breaks all year long.

Getting a group of kids together, it was easy to go "down to the river." When we were younger, we would play army, make lean-to forts out of limbs and sticks, catch rock bass, and play in the water, building small dams, or swimming. A couple of us were in the Boy Scouts and had camped there to earn our Polar Bear Badge for camping when the temperature was below freezing. As we got older, we would go down there, start little fires, and smoke cigarettes if we had any.

One particular evening, we headed down to one of our favorite spots. After we set up the tent on the riverbank side of the big sandbar, we started a fire closer to the water's edge and sat around talking. After an hour or so, one of my friends, whom I'll call Tim, decided to go up to the milk plant to get some sodas—pop, as we say in Minnesota—from a vending machine by the milk plant. If memory serves, Tim was initially going to head up alone, but I decided to go with him. I was surely thinking about safety in numbers when I started walking with him. As we headed toward the sole visible light pole, we watched carefully. It was completely dark, except for the faded orange glow of the streetlight, probably one hundred fifty yards away. With the fire making cracking sounds and our friends cracking jokes behind us at the campsite, we headed up toward the pop machine under the streetlight, believing everything would be all right. With three at the campsite and Tim and I together heading up to get pop, what could go wrong? With some soft yellow moonlight streaming through the trees and the fire throwing light from behind us, we could see well enough through the trees to walk without a flashlight. We knew this area like the back of our hands anyway.

As we walked off the sandbar, onto the riverbank, and into the more wooded area, we had to climb over many downed trees and through prickly bushes. Not 25 yards from the campsite, we came upon a very large tree that had fallen. As I recall, Tim went to the right, and I went more to the left, although it could have been the other way around. I may have been planning to walk around the uprooted side, but we spread apart by about half the length of the tree. He jumped up onto the trunk, which lay ominously in front of us like a barricade across a single road out of a fortified town under siege. It was at an angle but horizontal to the ground. As he hopped down from the tree trunk, Tim put his hand directly on a man's head. Crouched down behind the tree, Chester had waited. Turning back and screaming in a sound of guttural horror, Tim yelled, "There's a fucking guy out there and he's got a knife!" We raced back to the campsite, crashing through the woods and onto the sandbar. Our feet plunged into the soft sand like brakeless semis hitting a runaway truck ramp on a mountain. Literally fearing for our lives, we all huddled together, tried to calm down, and spoke quietly while trying to figure out how to take care of each other. We needed a plan. Leaving at that moment, grabbing our gear, and making a run for it was an option, but we had no way of knowing where Chester was. What if he stayed and was still there? Was he waiting for us to leave? None of us wanted our throats sliced. Another thought occurred to us: "Was there more than one guy in the woods?" The fear induced powerful stress. By this time, the boys in town were making guesses about whom the molester might be, but there was more than one possible suspect. We decided to make the fire much bigger, sit by it back to back, facing all directions with our knives brandished, and stay awake all night. At daylight, we would head home. It's still baffling why we'd even try camping during that time, but again; this may be a function of underdeveloped prefrontal cortexes.

Questions, fear, and anger raced through our minds. We kept our voices to a whisper for fear of Chester hearing us or us missing something—a sound or a sign of his presence. Our conversations were hushed, muffled, urgent, stressful. I had never been in a conversation like it, before or since. Each of us peered into the dark woods with intense and watchful eyes. We tried to be on high alert for the shadowy figure we had just encountered. Sitting near the fire, looking away from the woods, proved more difficult than being situated in the woods, peering into the light—like Chester was—but we had few options, given the circumstances. At most, there were two realistic ways to get in and out of there, and we knew that he knew them, too. What a harrowing night! Who was this? We wondered. Why did he come down there? Did he see the fire? Was he in Papa's Pizza? Did he hear us talking about going camping when we were downtown? Feelings of a turf war enveloped me because he had violated our space; this was our place to hang out, not his.

Once again, I was amazed that he would come after *us*. In this instance, there were five of us. Take a moment to think about that—five of us kids. Chester was an incredibly brazen predator. That night, I was the oldest in the group. I had played youth hockey with two of these kids; they were all a year behind me in school. In a way, I felt somewhat responsible for getting us all out of there safely in the morning. I was determined to do just that. While I know logically it was not the case, I had feelings of shame that Chester was really after me. Did I cause this? On some level, I thought or believed he was so infatuated with me that he followed us down there, and it was I who got us into this precarious predicament. One question I wondered but kept to myself was what Chester had actually planned to do before my friend literally stumbled onto him as he hid. Was he going to wait there until we went to sleep, then attack us? That is a disturbing thought.

Was he hoping one of us would wander off from the rest of the group at some point, like a lamb separated from the flock, only to be plucked off unexpectedly by a wolf, then molested, raped, or killed? Was he simply going to watch us? Would he sneak up and grope one of us, all of us? When the sun started to rise and the sky lightened, I felt grateful that he hadn't attacked us in the campsite through the night. I am not sure all of us stayed completely awake the entire time, but enough of us did to keep watch and maintain the fire. We were able to pack up our things and get out of there the next morning.

Surely, some readers wonder rightfully, "Who would let their children have so much freedom given the circumstances?" We can consider this from several angles. Some of my friends' parents may simply have been trusting of their boys. If we are not temporally centric, we can acknowledge that this was the case for many, probably most, families back then. Families let children do a lot more on their own than they do today. As you'll see later, our stories, and Jacob's in particular, played a large part in the subsequent changes we've seen in parenting. Even with all I've experienced, I often think the pendulum has swung too far in the other direction; now some children seem not to have the opportunity to talk to, or play with, children they do not know personally. We never had a play date; they did not exist. We played with whomever was around when we were. Times were different, but I will concede that many of us experienced a lack of parental supervision and did things, like staying out downtown later than we should have or that fateful camping trip, that put us in danger. Luckily, we got out of the situation without it worsening.

It may not have been the next morning, but at some point soon after that encounter, we tried to convince Tim to file a police report. He didn't want to go to the police, but I believe his grandmother eventually made him file it. I'm not sure why he didn't want to file one but have had my suspicions. He would never talk. The thought often occurred to me that maybe Tim actually knew all along who it was that night. Chester committed six other documented attacks during this period, besides the two I've described. Rumors suggest there were at least three other attacks or incidences too, one as late as 1991. To my knowledge, the victims didn't call the police, or if they did, the Paynesville Police Department destroyed the reports. Without a police report, the attacks are simply hearsay or urban legends, I realize. If the attacks didn't happen, the conversation about them shows how these attacks took on a life of their own in Paynesville, at least among some people.

Who is Chester?

Dangerous and unidentified, Chester moved stealthily on foot around Paynesville, creating a Yeti-like mystique—at least for us kids. We wanted to catch him to get our town back, along with our freedom. Seated behind the post office on the well-lit loading dock at night, Kirk and I used to talk about what was going on in town, what we could do to protect ourselves (sitting there at night probably was not the most enlightened choice—pun intended) and would discuss hypotheses about who Chester might be. We talked about this person because he was creepy, or that guy because he worked nights, or so-and-so because he knew all of us. We always kept a mental short list. In at least one other conversation with Kirk, he said he didn't believe the police would ever catch Chester. He suggested this mostly because the Paynesville Police Department didn't know how to deal with this type of crime and could not figure it out. He likened the Paynesville cases to a New York City crime with a Mayberry sheriff leading the investigation. These amateur sleuthing and friendly debate sessions took place after Chester's attack near my apartment in May 1987, up until about 1989. During that time, we focused on safety and survival, staying in tune with everything going on in town, and we attempted to identify Chester.

As mentioned, there was always speculation about who the masked molester was. One name invariably stayed on the short list: Duane Hart, also known as Dewey. Since he is a key component of the investigation of the crimes, I'll spend more time on Hart later, but he was a notorious pedophile in Paynesville. Well-known by many people in the area—adults and kids alike—Hart molested boys for decades, most often preying upon the Misfits. In a discussion about the night Chester came to the river, Tim—the boy who had put his hand on Chester's head when we were camping—was adamant it was not Duane Hart. Although intrigued and confused by his decisiveness—I had thought Hart was a prime suspect at that time—there was no reason to question Tim on this, I figured. Tim knew Hart. Sometimes, however, I wondered if Tim was using reverse psychology on us, saying it wasn't because it actually *was* Hart; but I wouldn't know his motivation for doing so. That statement probably sounds like I'm paranoid, and honestly, my hypothesis breaks down quickly when I try to generate reasons Tim would protect Hart. Hart was on people's radar, though. Admittedly, I was never sure how he felt so confident to rule Hart out that night, but he was certain. While people have reached out to Tim, now an adult, of course, he has always flatly refused to talk about the molester and this situation in particular—including the FBI. It has made me wonder if he was an abuse victim, perhaps one of Hart's. I will discuss Hart's role further in the book.

Except for one occasion, I never interacted with Hart, and even that one time in his presence, I did not speak to him directly, as far as I recall. On the eve of the fishing opener one year, while the Paynesville attacks were ongoing—I believe in 1988—several of us were hanging out in the evening. In Minnesota, the walleye season opens at midnight, typically on the Saturday of Mother's Day weekend. That night, Hart and his sidekick, whose name escapes me, had set up to fish from the shore on Lake Koronis, just outside Paynesville, southeast of town. Hart lived out that direction and had a shack, where, I believe, he probably molested boys. Later that night, while a group of us was driving around, it did not occur to me why we had stopped at Hart's fishing spot. We might have seen lights or perhaps someone in the car knew they were fishing down there. It's possible the driver was giving someone a ride who planned to fish with Hart and company. I can't remember that particular detail.

We parked and walked down to the lake's edge, standing around for about twenty minutes. Gratefully, that was the closest I ever got to Dewey Hart. Like most boys around my age in town, I had heard about him. Hart's piercing stare sent chills up and down my spine, and I knew there was no way I was staying there or ever being alone with him.

Call it a *Spidey Sense* or an intuitive thought or feeling, but it overpowered me; protecting myself became paramount. Some people give off a vibe that others notice. Of all the people I've ever been near, Hart was one of the creepiest.

Having never met the guy, I didn't process it in the moment, but looking back at that evening, the boys being around him for alcohol, drugs, or fishing trips made an impression on how I would later view him and his victims. I will discuss this in more detail in a later section. As it turned out, Hart was not the perpetrator of the Paynesville attacks, Jared's assault, or Jacob Wetterling's case, although Jacob's abduction and investigation provided the impetus for authorities to investigate Hart and for one of Hart's victims to come forward, detailing the abuse he caused.

CHAPTER 4
Living in Terror

If you're going through Hell, keep going.
~Winston Churchill

Stranger Attacks

In seeking safety away from home, I tried not to spend much time there. In doing so, I subjected myself to dangers I didn't fully understand—the terror going on in town. The word "molestation" doesn't do justice to what was going on in Paynesville; "attack" more accurately describes the abuse. The sexual attacks on boys began in 1986 when I was in seventh grade. Chester emerged from behind the trees after me in May of 1987, a few months later. I will never understand a couple of aspects of the Paynesville attacks. One is that, for a town of its size, an unbelievable number of adults—and even some children—never heard what was going on. This is despite some public attention from the school and law enforcement and the local newspaper, some of which I've included in this book. To put this in perspective, there are innumerable high schools with more students than the entire Paynesville community had residents. How did people miss it? Some of this could have been that adults, those whose children didn't experience the effects of

Chester's attacks, simply did not pay attention, but some of it surely had to be denial, too. After all, a crime like this in a small town is surely a cause for disbelief. In fairness, had I not been so involved in Chester's attacks, perhaps I would not have paid as much attention either. It's a bit of a stretch, but I suppose it's remotely possible children heard talk about "Chester the Molester" but didn't realize what was actually happening in town. For example, maybe they had heard the jokes and talk, but when it came right down to it, they didn't know it was real. Who would actually believe such a crazy thing happened in little Paynesville, anyway? Older children, those with cars, may not have been in touch as much either because they weren't really at risk like those of us who rode bikes. The school sent at least one notification home, and, as mentioned, Sergeant Drager had at least two articles in the paper.

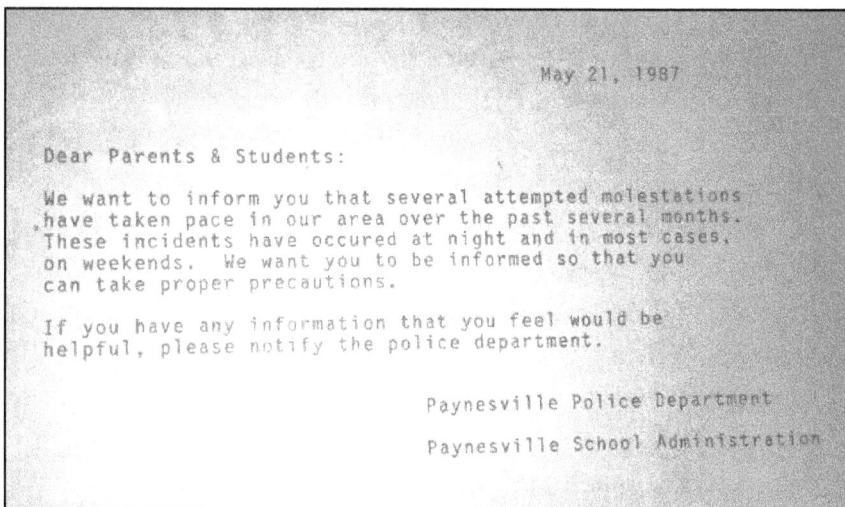

May 21, 1987

Dear Parents & Students:

We want to inform you that several attempted molestations have taken pace in our area over the past several months. These incidents have occured at night and in most cases, on weekends. We want you to be informed so that you can take proper precautions.

If you have any information that you feel would be helpful, please notify the police department.

Paynesville Police Department

Paynesville School Administration

Notification sent home with students following the attack on Kirk and me. May 16, 1987.

One concerned parent sent a letter to the editor as well. It's interesting to me how the children seemed either to know everything about Chester or to know nothing at all. The "Chester the Molester" comments were pervasive, yet some people who were even in the same class as the victims had no idea what the "Chester" moniker referred to—an actual molester. Recently, within the past few years, I have heard from parents who never knew what was going on back then. I find it astonishing. I've wondered how that's even possible.

In a town where the gossip got to the micro-level—where adults knew whose kids were smoking cigarettes behind a church—they somehow missed the news articles, letter to the editor, the urgent note from the school, or the talk around town about a *series* of violent attacks on boys by a child molester. I'm dubious of some of the claims of ignorance, but I guess it's possible. I'm not astonished about the victim shaming that went on in school; I'll never understand it, either.

As we know, schools can be havens for teasing, harassment, bullying, and the like. Children can be vicious. These days, technology and cyberbullying through social media may have supplanted some of the types of harassment that used to take place in school hallways, classrooms, and cafeterias. The amount of in-person bullying was probably worse back then than it is today. Paynesville was no different. It was clear whom the molester was stalking. He targeted the Misfits, mostly, those who spent time downtown, rode their bikes at night, and hung out by the river.

In school, some of the kids who knew about the attacks made jokes about them to the point of harassment. That behavior had started quite soon after the attacks began. For me personally, there were a few incidents where kids said they knew Chester was going to get me. There were a few kids, too, who recited a chant, "Chester's gonna get you... up the ass," which, of course, came too close to reality and was horrible to hear. If it was not bad enough living in the fear that Chester actually *was* going to get us, we had the added stress of dealing with harassment. I like to give people the benefit of the doubt, though. It's possible the bullying and harassing comments were a fear-based coping mechanism. After all, none of the kids knew who the molester actually was, let alone who was next. I'm guessing part of the reason the school and local law enforcement handled the cases the way they did is a function of the times and culture. Times were different, but I think most importantly, avoidance and a deep passivity, accompanied by denial, were exponentially stronger than today. It's a hunch, but I suspect the changes in schools resulted from harassment litigation, with the courts forcing school districts to assess themselves and provide a safe environment for students.

Today, if stranger accostings and molestations like these happened, I predict an extremely different response—more urgent and intense than it was back then. School psychologists, counselors, and social workers would likely be proactive, even getting assistance from neighboring schools. Social media would be abuzz with details, and people would raise awareness and disseminate information. Of course, the information would probably vary wildly, but it is more likely that people would know *something* was happening. In some ways, I believe the Paynesville Misfits, Jared Scheierl, and Patty Wetterling have affected some of these positive changes.

After Chester attacked Kirk the second time, I realized he was after me. The police report mentioned this too; it was easy to connect the dots. Because of where he was waiting—right by my apartment—and how quickly he let go of Kirk when he screamed at him, there was no doubt in our minds. The feelings associated with being *marked* were devastating. Chester intended to come after me by waiting to ambush me in view of my house while I was with Kirk. How disturbing and unbelievably brazen. He frequently attacked with more than one kid present. If he would come after kids in groups, what would stop him?

Filled with anger and fear after he grabbed Kirk, I decided I wasn't going down without a fight. If he grabbed me, I was prepared to stab him. He would have to kill me if it came to that; I lived on high alert. It became a matter of survival to protect myself and others from Chester. The Paynesville boys all had knives, and many of us had more than one. I made sure of that. After purchasing a heavy, silver-handled butterfly knife, I learned to open it quickly and was not afraid to use it. Living in constant fear, I tried to channel that fear into planning what I would do if attacked.

Taking it upon myself, I made it my duty and mission to ensure that boys younger than I knew they were at risk. I explained how they needed to take measures to protect themselves, and I wanted to help. Riding my bike, I carried my knife blade open, ready. Kirk had knives everywhere. He had them in his room, and when he started driving, he stashed them all over his car. We had collectively concluded that we were not putting up with the risk of Chester attacking us anymore, at least not without a fight. We had reached a high level of frustration, righteous indignation, and wanted to have a chance to get away, or at least inflict some damage back on Chester, if we had to do so. We figured if we stabbed him, someone would notice and ask him questions.

Over 25 years after the attacks, a man who had grown up in my part of town reached out to me via social media. A couple of years behind me in school, he shared how terrified he was when I explained to him and his friend that they needed to carry a knife to protect themselves. I had told him that neither the police nor anyone else would be able to help him if the molester grabbed him. In his low, raspy voice, the molester had told his victims he would kill them if they said anything or tried to get away. Threatening to take a child's life is incomprehensible and deplorable to me.

Living in Paynesville, never feeling safe, never knowing when Chester would grab me, was profoundly terrifying. It caused unbelievable, nearly unbearable stress. I had a paper route in upper elementary and middle school. It is disgusting to think about the fact that Chester seemed to have had a thing for paperboys. I rode my bike everywhere, including on my paper route. Along with me, one other Paynesville victim, Jared, and Jacob Wetterling were paperboys. Mostly because I spent so much time alone at night and because of the layout of where we lived, I began to engage in compulsive, exhausting mental gymnastics as coping mechanisms. Whether I started doing this when Chester attacked my friends, or later on, when he came after us from behind the pine trees, I don't know for sure, but it took up so much of my time and energy.

The common laundry room at the Black Saucer was directly under our apartment. Imagining Chester attacking me in vivid, frightening detail, I often pictured myself kneeling down, getting the clean clothes from the dryer and placing them in the laundry basket. Turning to my left and looking up, I would see him in the doorway, light streaming in from the streetlight behind him, his outline foreboding with his masked face—like looking up and seeing Michael Myers from the Halloween horror movie series. Unstoppable. Except this wasn't a movie. Adding to my fear and anxiety, our apartment door lock was not a deadbolt. In fact, it did not actually lock securely at all. It was a single-key lock without a deadbolt. By holding the doorknob and applying pressure from the left, you could move the latch bolt slightly. With a quick knee simultaneously to the right side of the door handle just below it, you could cause enough vibration to get the latch bolt over the strike. With this method, you could be in the apartment in seconds—without a key. Before Chester, this vulnerability wasn't an issue. Recall, this was small-town America.

When the attacks started, knowing how easily someone could get into the apartment damaged me psychologically. The high levels of cortisol in me all the time were unhealthy. Our landlord eventually replaced the door and lock, but fear had set in, living there, and the mind games I played to cope were in full effect. I would think to myself, *Just make it up the stairs in fewer than ten steps, and Chester won't get you.* Challenging myself, I often thought, *Oh, you didn't make it that time; do it again, or he will get you.* Another mind game I played was telling myself that if I could get the laundry out of the dryer and into the apartment in under a minute, I would be safe. I'd set the countdown timer on my Timex Ironman watch. Holding onto my dad's tattered, yellow plastic laundry basket just right so the clothes didn't fall out of the side with the split, I'd sprint up the stairs, trying to be safe, trying to make sense of this nonsense, trying to reconcile the experiences, and trying to exert some control over the uncontrollable. Attempting to manipulate cause and effect in this way was exhausting. I bit my nails down to nothing. The list goes on of the obsessive, albeit seemingly necessary, survival games I would play to distract myself from the fear. The games included counting, timing activities of all kinds, and little individual competitions. I'd set my watch to count down the school day or the number of hours until I got to do something fun, and then I'd test myself to avoid looking at the passage of time too frequently throughout a class or the school day.

While I logically knew these were simply mind games with no actual causal relationship to my experiences, they were coping mechanisms that helped me pass the time safely, soothing me to some extent. I felt so powerless in life. My obsessive mind games seemed to offer some short-term moments of relief. Even to this day, I sometimes catch myself counting steps or making sure that I get to the top of the stairs in seven or fewer steps. Later, I would turn to alcohol, but these games were a symbol of my commitment to myself to survive no matter what. Intent on making it through, I focused on coping; somehow, some way, I was going to be OK. Knowing I had friends helped too. I prayed for safety constantly.

Feeling Vulnerable

While some of the period is a blur, in many ways, 1986 to 1989 defined much of my life trajectory, at least for a while. One time, my dad and I went to church at the Newman Center at St. Cloud State University. A visiting Jesuit priest was there, and my dad thought it would be good for me to talk to him. Holding them in high regard, my dad had always spoken with admiration of the Jesuits. It was a good visit, as he was a younger priest who gave me suggestions about how to get away from Chester, how to protect myself, and so on. For example, he told me to take any measure to protect myself, including making noise, throwing something out the window—whatever it took. He was empathetic and understanding.

Fear ruled and lorded over me—a physical and cognitive response. When the days began to shorten in the fall of my ninth-grade year, I lived in abject terror that Chester would attack me before I got home or to my destination, wherever that might be. Not old enough to drive, I rode my bike everywhere in Paynesville. My dad worked the overnight shift, leaving me home alone from the time he went to work until he returned in the morning. Prior to Chester's attacks, this arrangement was tolerable; after all, I was a teenager and didn't mind being away from my dad. After he left for work, I often talked to friends on the phone, spending hours passing the time so I wouldn't feel alone. I frequently watched TV, sometimes into the wee hours, and then headed to bed. When my dad got home in the morning, he made sure I was ready for school and got me moving.

Chester had attacked a few kids by this point, including Kirk in February 1987; hearing about the attacks made me incredibly afraid and anxious. When Chester came after Kirk and me from behind the spruce trees, it created a nearly unbearable anxiety level. He had come after a group of five of us when we were camping, not to mention the other attacks. All bets were off after that camping trip. I had had enough and refused to stay home alone at night, only doing so when absolutely no alternative existed.

Starting with close friends, I began to shuffle around town from one friend's home to another, staying overnight and attending school with them in the morning. Many people in Paynesville let me stay with them on a rotating basis. Several friends accommodated me, but I felt like I was imposing. One elderly woman in particular, whom I'll call Mrs. Hanson, helped me immensely by letting me stay with her almost every night of the week during school. She was so kind, and I am grateful to have gotten to know her first by delivering her newspaper and later by having a safe place to stay. On a typical day, I would go to school, participate in sports practices during their respective seasons, and then head home. Later, in the evening, I would go to Mrs. Hanson's house. In the morning, I would eat breakfast with her, and my dad would pick me up after work. We would head over to the apartment where I would get ready for school. There were many kind people in Paynesville, including one family in particular who helped immensely.

CHAPTER 5
Getting Through

There is nothing on this earth more to be prized than true friendship. ~Thomas Aquinas

By eighth grade, my life felt like it was in a full-blown tailspin. People in Paynesville showed me love, kindness, and patience; they cared for me. One of the first people I met in Paynesville was Matt. His dad, Roy, a local banker, helped my dad with banking. My dad knew him through doing business there. Roy's son, Matt, and I were the same age and inseparable for years. We did everything together, including playing games outside, like *Kick the Can,* building snow forts in winter, playing sports, trading baseball cards, going out to eat at Tuck's Café or the Wishing Well in downtown Paynesville. I would often stay over at their place.

We'd impersonate the McKenzie Brothers from the 1980s movie *Strange Brew* in our best nasally Canadian accents: "Hey, hoser," "Take off, eh," and Elvis, "Thank ya, thank ya very much." We hunted together. We'd rent movies, just like Jacob and his friends were doing. Back in those days, when VCRs first came out, they were too expensive for most people to buy. We'd have to rent one of those as well, lugging the machine and cables home in its huge, zippered, soft-sided case resembling a giant pizza delivery bag. Matt's family took me in like one of their own. Roy and Mary, Matt's parents, were kind and loving people. I viewed them as normal, an excellent contrast to my own home life with my dad, which was anything but normal. Matt's siblings were good to me, too, treating me like one of their own and serving as role models and an adoptive family.

They demonstrated what family life could be like, providing stability and safety when I was with them. Staying at their house innumerable times, I frequently started or spent my weekends there, lounging around on Saturday mornings. On snow days from school, I'd ride my bike over in the morning and spend the whole day. If the district canceled school the evening before, I'd go to their house to spend the night so I'd already be there. We'd hang out in their basement, eating Doritos (Cool Ranch came out in 1986) and Funyuns. We'd watch movies and play video games, and in the morning, Matt's mom would come down to see chip bags, soda cans, and boys in sleeping bags strewn all over the basement floor. With Matt's family, I always felt—and still feel—like a member. As an only child, he and his siblings were like my own.

A couple of years before the attacks in Paynesville began, Matt's sister lost her life in a car accident. I felt such deep loss and such profound sadness for their family. The way everyone supported each other during that difficult time was remarkable. Deep sorrow filled their faces, and I can still envision the graveside service, picturing Roy and Mary holding each other, their heads touching together as they stood by their daughter's casket. I started to believe that if their family could get through the terrible experience of losing their daughter, I could use their resolve as an example. Experiencing this stalking of my friends and myself and losing a child so tragically are obviously nowhere near the same, but some of the requisite pieces are similar: the same love, understanding, support for one another, patience, friendship, and faith. The experience had deepened my respect for them. It drew me closer than ever and, I believe, to some degree, served to strengthen my own persistence and resilience later in life, especially when the attacks started.

Strength, Persistence, and Grit

I've since learned that healthy relationships heal trauma[3], and that is precisely what my friends were doing for me. I am living proof, along with countless others, that it is possible to make it through terrible circumstances and come out of them, intact. I believe our life outcomes result partially from our environment, partly from genetics, and partly from the choices we make. Gratefully, in my case, I had enough positive people and influences in my life to outweigh the negative impacts. My friendships helped me develop a presence of mind and a consciousness that steered me in a positive direction, which would otherwise not have been possible had my home environment been my only

---

[3] Bessel Van der Kolk, *The Body Keeps the Score: Brain, Mind, and Body in the Healing of Trauma*. New York: Viking, 2014.

influence. People like Matt and his family buoyed me through some of the most unbelievable times in my life.

Lifelong friends Matt and I have maintained our strong friendship throughout marriages, kids, career changes, and more, staying in contact and getting together whenever possible.

Matt has always been a person with whom I can check in, and vice versa, running things by one another because we have a common history, background, and understanding. I've tried to incorporate this steadfast loyalty into new friendships over the years, too.

Being available, being accountable to one another, and having a person to turn to, I believe, literally kept me from going crazy. My friendship with Matt and with some others in Paynesville helped me get through a couple of the most terrifying, darkest years of my life.

CHAPTER 6
Enough is Enough

Wherever I go, there I am. ~Anonymous

Ninth Grade and the Move

Like me, my dad was battling some issues when I was in ninth grade. With his work situation causing unbearable stress, my dad slid into an abysmal state of depression, which manifested in the form of sleeping almost around the clock, unless it was necessary for him to get up. Depression can overwhelm. I would stay home a lot, simply paralyzed emotionally. Not all kids growing up in difficult circumstances, or dealing with trauma, make bad choices regarding school or work. While uncommon, there are examples of kids who, despite the most deplorable situations, excel in school. I wasn't one of them. Many more do not excel, instead following a family's patterns and cycles of violence, often with negative outcomes. The effects of being in a constant fight-or-flight state because of Chester chasing us took its toll. Finding it virtually impossible to concentrate, I used whatever I could to stay home or leave school early.

Being in such constant fear and with the exhaustion caused by trying to maintain an image of having everything together took its toll on me mentally and physically. The result was the same, though: missing school was a source of all kinds of academic problems. Knowing I didn't have my work done, always being behind because I wasn't there, and not being able to focus when I was in school posed difficulties in several ways, including some legal trouble.

Juvenile Court

Having never heard anyone use the phrase "troubled kid" to my face, I'm not sure if my teachers or administrators in school ever officially deemed me to be in that category, but without question, I was on the precipice and slipped over the edge at least temporarily one time. While in the throes of the Chester attacks, I had been hanging around with some friends during my ninth-grade year. It may have been homecoming, but I know we had been at school, perhaps at a volleyball game or varsity football game. I had not been playing varsity then. We dropped off one or two of our friends at their parents' farm places and, in hindsight, it's unfortunate that I had seen the movie *Stand by Me* recently and got the bright idea to play mailbox baseball. My friends didn't talk any sense into me, or if they did, I invoked my exceptional leadership skills and convinced them. Getting a bat from our friend when we dropped him off at his place, the rest of us went driving all around the township wrecking people's mailboxes. While we made a stupid choice, we didn't actually intend to hurt anyone or violate the people whose property we destroyed, even though that is exactly what we did. We had stopped at the Hilltop Restaurant after our ill-chosen adventure. We must have been talking about it, not surprisingly, and the police caught us. Charged with the offense, we went to juvenile court. Arriving early, we met with a public defender. With no intention of denying what I had done, I was prepared to take responsibility and punishment.

Appearing before the judge in my gray, three-piece suit from the Salvation Army thrift store, I can still remember having had the arm length and pants altered to fit properly; however, the fit of the jacket and pants was baggy, making me feel even more awkward than usual. Scared to death because I was not some hardened criminal without a conscience, I will never forget how the judge began. He asked me what position I played in baseball. Answering him, "Second base and catcher, Your Honor," he followed up by asking if I wanted to play baseball for a different school the next year—thus informing me, albeit in a passive-aggressive way, that he had the authority to send me away. My friends were all in Paynesville; it was what I knew. In juvenile court, judges adjudicate cases with the hope that the kids do not return for additional offenses, which I did not. Receiving probation and being ordered to make restitution, that summer I got a job and earned enough to pay for the damages I had caused and went personally to each of the homeowners, apologizing for my actions. I had made a poor choice with my friends, and we had damaged people's property. When law enforcement caught us, we experienced the consequences of that choice.

Essentially incapacitated emotionally and unable to continue working at his place of employment, my dad wanted to move. He arranged to take an early retirement. The plan was to move to St. Cloud, MN, from Paynesville upon completion of my first year of high school. He had reasons for wanting to leave his job, and it worked out well for me, as I could not bear to live any longer in the stress of wondering if Chester would continue to stalk my friends and me. Excited and grateful to be getting away from the terror, and transferring to a new school to start my sophomore year, St. Cloud seemed to be a wonderful idea. This was an opportunity to escape from Paynesville and, more specifically, Chester, with the bonus of a larger city with many more people and more things to do. With my youthful naivety, it felt like a change that had the potential to bring the peace that I had longed for so long. We would finally be able to live like a "normal" family. It seemed "normal" would be without my dad working at night and me not living in constant fear of Chester.

To St. Cloud

The financial nature of taking an underfunded early retirement affected the timing and logistics of our move from Paynesville to St. Cloud. School started for me after Labor Day, but for things to work out financially, my father had to work until the end of the year, if I remember correctly. We had been attending church in St. Cloud for a couple of years and knew some people in the parish. After asking around for help, my dad found a nice couple with two children who had an extra room where I could stay during the week, so I didn't have to start school and then switch soon after. My dad paid for room and board, so I was able to move before him and start school.

Once school started in St. Cloud, I tried to live in such a way—or at least create an illusion—that I had a normal life to forget about Chester. Of course, the reality of Heinrich attacking my friends and me had affected me profoundly. Trying to avoid and escape, I joined every club I could think of at school, went to church, and was involved with volunteering there, and got a part-time job. For the most part, I got along with everyone at the new school, but it was still difficult because of all I hadn't dealt with personally. Maintaining the incongruent interior and exterior was the worst part. Being a kid full of fear and lacking insight, I didn't know help might be available, or how to get it. For many years, I struggled with the notion that I didn't want to be who I was. I longed to be a different person, to have a different life. With this feeling came a sense that conditions, situations, and people could affect one's state of being—happy, joyous, and free. My dad worked hard but made little income. Naively, I would wonder if more income might make it better for him.

In St. Cloud, I got a job washing dishes and bussing tables at a popular Mexican restaurant on Mall Germain downtown. The place was known for its fried ice cream and giving customers a free meal on their birthday. It had a stucco interior with enclosed booths, each with an arch and brightly colored paint. As a kid, I had eaten there innumerable times with my dad. It was a favorite of mine, and working there gave me a sense of connection to the place, but I confess, I entered the job in complete disillusionment over what working as a dishwasher and bussing tables in a restaurant would be like. Restaurant work is not for the weak. These days, having worked in the restaurant business at low-level jobs more than once, I tip well and treat staff with extra kindness. Working the closing shift meant we couldn't leave until everyone was out of the restaurant; we had to get all the work done, with no dishes left behind. It required teamwork on the part of the *dish crew* to get things done quickly, or we'd have to stay late.

Just like in Paynesville, I rode my bike everywhere in St. Cloud. Some nights I'd get a ride home from one of the people with whom I worked at the restaurant, but if not, I rode home as fast as I possibly could. The sense of fear and panic as I rode from the restaurant after work at night was similar to that in Paynesville. The stress of trauma wired itself into my mind and body so that I was in a state of fight, flight, or freeze all the time. The move to St. Cloud was supposed to be a fresh start and a safer place. It wasn't long until that changed.

CHAPTER 7
Jared Scheierl, Jacob Wetterling, and Paynesville

The obscure we see eventually. The completely obvious, it seems, takes longer. ~Edward R. Murrow

I n this chapter, I'm going to share my perspective on events as I saw and felt them. Later, I'll revisit several aspects of the cases and discuss what I have learned since law enforcement solved them. It's important to note that much of what I share is from my perspective as a middle to early high school student trying to navigate life under tremendous stress. Looking back, after much therapy and reflection, I see and think differently than I did in real time.

Jared Scheierl: You Can't Make This Up

Jared's story can leave people speechless. Living in Cold Spring, MN, at the time, eighteen miles from Paynesville, Jared was walking home after being with his friend when a car stopped and the driver asked him where a local family lived. Jared told him. The man got out, told Jared to get into the car, and drove Jared out of town, where he stopped and then sexually assaulted him. The man told Jared he knew all his family. He said, "I know who you are and where you live." The man told Jared that he could talk about what happened, but that if authorities ever got close to finding out who he was, he would come back and kill Jared. He took some of Jared's clothing—trophies—and made Jared get out of the car and run home in nothing but his snowmobile suit in January in Minnesota. When Heinrich released Jared, he said, "Now run; don't look back, or I'll shoot." Jared got home shaken and understandably hysterical. His family contacted the police, and the officer took his statement, beginning the investigation into Jared's assault.

Cold Spr:

COLD SPRING, MI

Crime Stoppers
Needs Public's Information

[4]Cold Spring Record

---

[4] Cold Spring Record Article. Cold Spring Record, "Crime Stoppers Needs Public's Information," (Cold Spring, MN), Feb. 7, 1989.

Jacob Taken, October 22, 1989

I'm able to feel a physical response to this day whenever I think of it; the chills start in my shoulders. They start predominantly on the outside, work their way down my arms, and continue throughout the rest of my body. I will never forget my reaction when I heard about Jacob Wetterling's abduction from quaint, little St. Joseph, Minnesota, on October 22, 1989. Walking west along St. Germain Street in downtown St. Cloud on an unusually warm fall day, a frantic young woman ran up to me, handed me a flier with Jacob's picture on it, and said a man had pulled Jacob off his bike the night before and taken him. Having flashbacks in that moment, I returned mentally to Paynesville. Believing it might have been the same man who had stalked, terrorized, and preyed on us young boys in Paynesville a couple of years earlier, I remember thinking viscerally, "My God, not again." After hearing more details on the news and reading about how it had happened, I saw the crimes were frighteningly similar. I distinctly remember thinking to myself that the very reason I wanted to move to St. Cloud was to get away from this. I was incensed. The details hit close to home: this was another group of boys riding their bikes at night, the surprise attack, all of it. To me, these crimes related to each other in some way, no question. In fact, looking at them on the surface, it took effort to find the differences because the similarities were so striking. Not to sound like a conspiracy theorist or cynical this early, but I wondered whether anyone could really believe there was an entire group of pedophiles in the area.

I had just turned 16 years old, as mentioned, completely filled with fear and anxiety most of the time. It was difficult to get through each day. I had put on a false smile and a false persona by this point in my life, but Jacob's abduction heightened my fear and anxiety tremendously.

The primary reason I wanted to move to St. Cloud was to escape the terror of living in Paynesville and, more specifically, the constant threat of Chester targeting me and my friends. Going to the police was very difficult, as it made me vulnerable to an authority. Overwhelmed with the suspicion that the crimes were connected—and that perhaps the same person was responsible for the attacks in Paynesville and Jacob's disappearance—I contacted the Stearns County Sheriff's Department. I met with a detective who took my statement.[5] He told me he would pass the information along to the investigation team, which they called the *Jacob Wetterling Task Force* at that time. Waiting anxiously, I expected to hear from someone soon—another officer, or maybe the FBI. I wanted to help, to make a difference, and to matter. What we experienced in Paynesville was part of me, still unresolved and incredibly fresh.

---

[5] Stearns County Sheriff's Office, "Case # 89006407 Wetterling Homicide case files" (St. Cloud, MN 2018).

DATE: _102489_   TIME: _1540_   STATUS: A (B) C

OPERATOR: _T.Lim_

SOURCE OF INFORMATION:

NAME: _KRIS ALLEN BERTELSEN, DOB 011903_   WORK PHONE: _____
ADDRESS: _921 6TH AVE SO_ _ST CLOUD, MN_   HOME PHONE: _259-980_

INFORMATION: _HE STATED THAT ABOUT 2 YEARS AGO_
THERE WERE 7 TO 9 ATTEMPT/MOLESTATIONS
IN PAYNESVILLE — "INCIDENTS OCCURRED
AT NIGHT" SGT BELL DAMER,
PAYNESVILLE POLICE INVESTIGATED
THE CASE. HE IS TRYING IT IS
CONNECTED TO OUR CASE.

SUSPECT: NAME: _DOUG FLINT_ TELEPHONE: _____
ADDRESS: _____
EMPLOYER: _____
DOB: _____ AGE: _____
VEHICLES: LIC: _____ STATE: _____
HT: _____ WT: _____ HAIR: _____

ASSIGNED TO: _Bregan_   DATE: _____ TIME: _____

RESULTS: _____
_____
_____

Over period of 1 year, 6 to 7, 12 to 13 yr olds
boys may have been abused.

see also 277, 294, 446, 475, 2448

My tip to the Stearns County Sheriff's Department, submitted
within 48 hours of Jacob's abduction 10-24-1989.

After Jacob's abduction, central Minnesota was in a frenzy. It was *the* news story. As you can imagine or remember, it was gripping, riveting, and so very wrong. On every media outlet I came across, Jacob's story was there, captivating and unheard of. People were, I believe, dumbfounded and mesmerized by its occurrence, especially in such a rural area. This kind of thing just doesn't happen in central Minnesota. Sometimes, resentment boiled up as I listened to interviews or read articles about Jacob, reflecting on what we went through in Paynesville. It didn't seem as surprising to the Misfits in Paynesville. Filled with anger over what had happened to Jacob, I wanted desperately for him to come home safely, to help if I could, and to bring Chester to justice.

Did They Get My First Tip?

From October 24, 1989—when I first talked to the Stearns County Sheriff's Department about the possible connections— until December, I hadn't heard back. The Stearns County deputy who took my statement said the Jacob Wetterling Task Force would contact me.

While I had no doubt about their good intentions, they never did follow through. It left me with a most troubling, unsettling feeling. My eye twitched, and my stomach turned as I worried about Jacob and the Misfits, wondered what had happened, and hoped for someone to ask about the Paynesville cases. I didn't know what to expect, and I'm not exactly sure what I had in mind. At the very least, though, I expected someone from Stearns County to follow up with a phone call, take a statement, or maybe ask me for more names of Paynesville victims. Knowing the severity of the crime and the size of the investigation, I tried to be patient, giving law enforcement the benefit of the doubt. Charlie Graft was the Stearns County Sheriff at that time, and I don't question his administration and his own personal desire to solve the case and bring Jacob home. As time has gone by, I don't recall if I followed up with Stearns County in the two months between my first tip and the next tip, but it is possible I called to check with them. The original statements from Paynesville, and my lead, helped to finally catch the perpetrator in 2016.

I have learned that it's easier to try to work with people and get along with them than to be antagonistic. In the investigation of Jared's case (which I didn't know much about yet at this time, and will discuss shortly) and Jacob's disappearance, there didn't seem to be any purpose or benefit gained early on from criticism or cynicism. We Misfits wanted to help. The people in communities all around the area wanted to help. We were all trying to head in the same direction, to get Jacob home. Honestly, the tips and information from us and Jared's horrific experience and cooperation with the investigation, coupled with some striking, disturbing similarities between all the cases, seemed obvious. However, after reading the case files, there are reasons it wasn't easy to solve, not the least of which was the sheer volume of tips coming in from all over. I saw no reason not to trust the investigators, but to me back then, the case seemed locked up because they were getting so much information. Over time, information inundated officials, as I heard. I assumed they were doing their best trying to follow up on leads and tips to catch whoever took Jacob. I try to give people the benefit of the doubt. As time passed, though, I found the law enforcement officials' lack of follow-through frustrating. I felt they weren't interested in our ideas or possible leads. At the very least, I believed they weren't following up in the way that I thought they should be, especially because they hadn't contacted me, which I admit, probably sounds pompous.

Watching the news, reading the paper, and seeing law enforcement officials follow leads and come up short, I became increasingly frustrated. Some of the tips and leads I heard about seemed preposterous, especially compared to the believable, and, in my opinion, undeniable, similarities to the tip I had given them. It felt to me almost as if they were seeking reasons for it *not* to be the same perpetrator as opposed to connecting the dots. Frustration ensued for what turned into years, then decades. I'd catch myself saying, "Go to Paynesville!" This is not to suggest I *knew* law enforcement officials and investigators were wrong or not trying; I didn't. In my original tip, I gave them a possible name and described the attacks I knew about in detail. Obviously, the Paynesville attacks were in close proximity to St. Joseph and Cold Spring, the ages of the kids were close, and several aspects of the cases were hauntingly, disturbingly similar. In the Paynesville and Wetterling cases, it was especially noteworthy that we were in groups and riding bikes. The investigation quickly sprawled all over the country. I would hear about the search for Jacob—the largest of its kind—and how they were following up on leads. Law enforcement has to do so, and, as I mentioned, the volume of them was incredible. It's also unfortunate that the investigation scaled up to what I believed to be vast geographic proportions. Some would argue that Paynesville was too far away as well. Even given what they knew about Heinrich, Hart, and what we knew and shared about Paynesville, law enforcement officials couldn't get the evidence needed to arrest and convict Heinrich when investigating Paynesville originally.

Understandably overshadowed by Jacob Wetterling's abduction, law enforcement and media separated and shifted away from the Paynesville victims and their stories, perhaps assuming there was no relationship between the cases or, at the very least, there was no evidence of a relationship. Of course, we know now that moving away from Paynesville was incorrect. There are exceptions, but my experience with the Stearns County Sheriff's Department was that they were simply not open to communication, at least not with me about the case. I'm sure that position is a policy, but my teenage brain wasn't having it.

With possible connections to Jacob, I tried to get the Stearns County Sheriff's officials to listen to me. It also had to do with my desire for justice for what we had experienced in Paynesville. The investigation of the Paynesville molestation cases did not yield an arrest and conviction in Jacob's case. To my knowledge, Stearns County had not previously conducted an investigation into our cases, but the FBI had. It occurred to me that if the abduction of a child could not get Stearns County to focus on what happened in Paynesville, nothing would. Believing that Stearns County would thoroughly investigate our cases in Paynesville because of the possibility of a connection to Jacob, I paid close attention to the news. I was persistent and wanted Stearns County officials to take us seriously. I assumed the gravity of someone abducting a child in such a strikingly similar way to the multiple attacks in Paynesville would prompt urgency on law enforcement's part. This is not to say that investigators were not working behind the scenes. I know they were. They arrested a notorious predator because of the Paynesville information and the courage of one of his victims who came forward.

I assumed the Wetterling tragedy would put the Paynesville cases at the forefront of the investigation. After all, Jacob was gone. Furthermore, I believed someone could solve our cases, perhaps even as an externality—a positive spillover effect—of the Wetterling investigation. Back then, at least initially, I believed they would find Jacob alive quickly and return him to his family. I hadn't heard back about my tip to law enforcement, so in December 1989, taking it upon myself, I had my dad make an appointment with Jerry Wetterling's chiropractic office. It may seem odd to approach him to talk about the abduction of his son, but going to their home or calling didn't seem right.

Directly to Jerry Wetterling

Jerry Wetterling had just returned when we went to see him in December 1989. He had taken time off from work after Jacob's abduction. The ostensible reason for our visit was a chiropractic adjustment for my dad. In reality, I wanted to make sure he, and law enforcement, knew about the Paynesville cases. A couple of months had gone by since I reached out to Stearns County. I thought to myself, "This tip is hot!" and I wanted to make sure Jerry knew about our experiences in Paynesville. The investigation had not yielded a conclusion to the Paynesville cases, and Jacob was still missing. I felt compelled to go directly to Jacob's father. After all, the passage of time made it seem they would soon lose any traction the investigation might have had. Did it help to sit around any longer? Speaking up, making oneself vulnerable, calling for attention and action, but feeling unheard or ignored, invokes a most painful, deafening silence.

I thought the cases were connected and that Jerry's influence would get something going in Paynesville; I felt it was the right thing to do. Besides, by ignoring me—intentionally or not—law enforcement was reinforcing a message that I didn't matter, making me persist even more. The *not knowing* was the source of frustration for me, and I'm taking the liberty to speak for the Misfits in Paynesville to say they felt the same. The waiting, the silence, with no resolution had lasting consequences on many people, and this includes members of law enforcement. When you read and hear people speak about why they were angry about the Wetterling investigation, I believe this is often why. The unknown can make people search for someone to blame, too, and in this case, I think that was law enforcement.

Meeting with Jerry was surreal. His nurse sent us back to the room, and he came in a few minutes later. Seeing him for the first time, my initial feeling was relief and my thoughts hopeful: "Maybe we can help each other." Jerry was tall and thin, with a calm, caring demeanor. He was interested in what I had to share, and I began nervously describing the Paynesville attacks. He listened intently, and I felt his sincerity. Our conversation went smoothly. Having no reason to feel any different, I left there with a new optimism, a feeling of relief that maybe we could put all of this to rest, and truly believed it was possible. I assumed that he and Patty had heard thousands of leads and tips. I'm speculating, but he and Patty probably had to be cautious not to get their hopes up too soon when the tips came in. I remember hearing about how their home phone number was a sort of tip line. The calls would come to their home whenever. That would never happen today.

As I had done when I contacted Stearns County right after I heard about Jacob, I told Jerry about the Paynesville attacks in as much detail as I could remember. There were thousands of tips coming in from all over the country during the investigation, but again, I really believed mine was hot—a tip they could not miss nor ignore. Apparently, everyone thought his or her tip was hot. As mentioned, the case files are immense. I gave Jerry names of others to speak with in Paynesville. It wasn't long after I spoke to Jerry for the first time that investigators interviewed some Paynesville people.

It is likely the case that law enforcement was already investigating Paynesville when I went to Jerry, but I am still glad I did it. First, I believe our meeting helped lay some of the groundwork for law enforcement to solve the cases later; second, I had the privilege of meeting one of the nicest people.

Heinrich Interviewed

Filled with hope, I got my expectations up, along with feelings of accomplishment and pride, that justice would prevail. A glimmer of hope shone through in the investigation when I heard that the FBI had become significantly involved. To me, the FBI meant serious business. It conjured up images of getting things done, taking names, and making arrests. The FBI sent agents to Paynesville High School; they interviewed some of the boys involved. That action, I believed, could be a turning point, not only in Jacob's disappearance but also in ensuring that our cases would get the attention they deserved. I often wondered what it would take to get law enforcement really involved in catching Chester, and now the FBI was in Paynesville. Having experienced and seen the effects firsthand, I wanted justice served. I never thought anyone at the Paynesville Police Department shirked his or her responsibilities; I just believed they lacked the resources and expertise to deal with this type of crime. After nearly three years of hell, I hoped we might be able to find out who Chester really was and bring him to justice. On some level, the longing for justice must be in the back of every crime victim's mind.

Without knowing everything going on behind the scenes, I didn't feel the law enforcement investigators took us seriously. I know some others felt this way too. It is possible, even likely, that I am wrong, but that was the feeling. When the perpetrator abducted Jacob, I struggled with worry, wondering what had happened to him, where he was, hoping he was safe, but fearing otherwise. Even though Jacob and I never met, I always felt a connection to him because of the bikes, because of the modus operandi, and because of the crime. Hope gave way to frustration quite quickly. Living in St. Cloud at that time, I didn't have the same level of connectedness to Paynesville as before—this was several years before cell phones proliferated society, and I always wondered what happened in Paynesville. Law enforcement interviewed Heinrich, whom I didn't know personally and didn't know was a suspect. Chief Schmiginsky went to Stearns County. From the outside peering in on the investigation, there didn't seem to be any other options but for us to trust and hope for the best.

Giving up entirely was an option, too, which is ultimately what I did, but not without first trying. When I gave Stearns County the tip on October 24, and when I went to Jerry's office in December 1989, I had mentioned Hart by name as a suspect in Paynesville and Jacob's disappearance. Authorities arrested, charged, and convicted Hart of molesting boys in the Paynes-ville area when one of his victims came forward.[6]

The Paynesville Press

Tuesday, January 30, 1990
Volume 103, Number 9
Copyright 1990, The Paynesville Press

35¢
Serving the Paynesville area for 102 years

Charged with molesting boys
Belgrade man arrested

By Tim Douglass

'We definitely know there are more victims out there...'
""

Hart and Heinrich, who apparently were friends with affinities for boys, were both located in Paynesville. The Paynesville attacks stopped after Hart's arrest, presenting an unbelievable, cruel irony that not one but two predators were in Paynesville.

------

[6] Tim Douglass, "Charged with Molesting Boys, Belgrade Man Arrested." *Paynesville Press*, January 30, 1990.

It also seems, in hindsight, that Hart's reputation allowed Heinrich to continue his actions, almost as though Hart was involuntarily running interference for Heinrich.

Not Feeling Safe

Trying to start over in Paynesville and the Chester attacks were not topics I ever brought up to my classmates at the new school in St. Cloud. Keeping these secrets made functioning normally on any level extremely difficult. My attempts to prevent the thoughts and emotions of my experiences from controlling me proved to be easier said than done. Sitting at the lunch table, for example, when kids would talk about a dance, sporting event, pretty girls, or whatever, I tried to pay attention and engage, but I struggled to do so as the feelings of fear and uncertainty from Chester stalking us affected me.

My friend, whom I'll call Jake, was in the high school band with me and always reached out to me and tried to be my friend, despite my incredible mood swings. I was aware during that time that I had mood swings; I just found it impossible to stop—impossible to stop thinking about my experiences in Paynesville, once the thoughts took over. We had some classes together. Both trumpet players, we played in the pep band at various sporting events. We did the normal things high school kids do, but for me, it always felt—and perhaps was—different. Sitting in a gym full of people, for example, I would wonder if Chester was still chasing boys at knifepoint and still looking for me, and I was usually preoccupied with it. I never felt safe. Wanting friends, I tried to maintain a façade. Wanting to be included, I tried to pretend nothing was wrong, that I was just like most of them: a happy, regular kid, but with powerful, inescapable strength, like the undertow in a river—fear and negativity never left my mind. I developed unshakable anxiety and began to avoid things. Rather than dealing with things like schoolwork directly, I would procrastinate or avoid them altogether, often to the point of missing deadlines and shirking responsibilities. I was unreliable, but I didn't feel safe telling anyone why.

My schoolwork and scores again started to decline precipitously at the second school. Predictably, I started missing many days of school, and I did poorly. Assignments piled up, and in true avoider form, the bleaker the outlook, the more I avoided the issues. I exceeded the permissible number of days absent for the semester, and the school ultimately gave me some choices, but staying there any longer wasn't one of them. I could leave that school for another school or attend an alternative center. If I didn't take them up on one of those options, they would kick me out, but either way, I was done. I had never talked to any school officials about the attacks in Paynesville, and school officials never asked. There were no interventions, no meetings, just an ultimatum. The way the school officials handled my situation wasn't good for me, and I'm hopeful things have changed. I didn't fight their decisions because it was true that I had missed the days and was getting behind. Fighting this would have required me to open myself up, to being vulnerable and explaining what had gone on in Paynesville. Still reeling from the aftermath of all I had experienced in Paynesville, I wasn't in an emotional place to be able to do it. Missing my friends anyway, I left St. Cloud for half of my eleventh-grade year and for my entire senior year. I drove back and forth from St. Cloud to Paynesville.

Paynesville Classmates, but Anonymously

In a bone-chilling irony, Jared Scheierl moved to Paynesville a couple of months after I had moved away to St. Cloud. Jared and I moved for the exact same reason: to get away from the perpetrator who had respectively caused so much hell. Prior to Jacob Wetterling's disappearance, I had never heard of Jared Scheierl's case. Seeing the police sketch artist's rendition of the attacker from Jared's description, I remember thinking to myself, "How in the world did Jared and I not know about this? How did we never talk about this at school?"

In order to protect his identity during the Wetterling investigation, the media reported abstractly about Jared, referring to him as "a 12-year-old boy from Cold Spring, MN." As I discussed previously, the school gave me an ultimatum. Not wanting to start over again in yet another St. Cloud school, I returned to Paynesville midway through my junior year, where I had met Jared but didn't know much about him. I knew Jared and "a 12-year-old from Cold Spring" as separate people and situations, not as one and the same. Jared and I knew all the same families. We had many friends in common, yet none of them—nor he and I—had connected our stories back then. To this day, I can't believe some of those mutual friends didn't sit each of us down and talk about our respective stories. The "Chester" narrative was well-known among kids in Paynesville. Jared shared his story with some of his friends, but nobody thought to connect Jared and me until the late 2000s. One of Jared's closest friends lived at the house on the corner where Heinrich came running after us in May 1987. It's unfathomable to me still.

I find it incredible how Jared's kidnapping and assault—as well as our cases—did not make bigger news. In such rare crimes, one would think alarms would have sounded long before Heinrich took Jacob. After Jacob's abduction, law enforcement zeroed in on Jared, interviewing him multiple times, perhaps to the point of interrogating him, which ultimately led to his family's decision to move. Law enforcement explored possible connections to the cases[7]. At the time we attended high school together in Paynesville, I never spoke to Jared about the Paynesville attacks, and obviously, he didn't share what had happened to him.

One person, Danny Heinrich, was a suspect in Jared's assault early on—even back then—and I knew nothing about Jared or Danny Heinrich. I'll spend more time connecting a few dots and tying up loose ends regarding the cases later, but the burden of identifying his attacker must have been tremendous. Law enforcement never conducted a lineup for the Paynesville victims. I have always believed there should have been communication between two small towns 18 miles apart in such rare cases. If, in fact, the departments did communicate, it did not work to catch the perpetrator, unfortunately.

---

[7] Kirsten Haukebo, "Two Abductions May Be Linked." *St. Cloud Times*, December 14, 1989. https://www.newspapers.com/article/st-cloud-times/136435741/

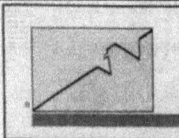

© St. Cloud Times – USA TODAY NETWORK

It always seemed to me that Paynesville was too small for someone not to know something about the attacks, yet to my knowledge, nothing came out. Sergeant Drager worked hard to keep the kids alert and safe. It has been my long-held belief that the crimes could have been stopped in Paynesville—that someone knew. One of those someones could have been Paynesville Police Chief Robert Schmiginsky, who went to Stearns County with a tip—naming Danny Heinrich as a suspect in the Paynesville attacks—right after I reached out to them the second time. Perhaps close to catching Heinrich in Paynesville, Schmiginsky went to the Task Force on January 8, 1990. Any reasonable person would ask, "What made Heinrich a suspect?" Without access to notes or Paynesville records, and coupled with the late Chief Schmiginsky's absolute refusal to speak about the cases, there may be no way of really getting the desired answers. Obviously, Schmiginsky knew something or had an intuitive hunch about Heinrich. It was a good thing that Schmiginsky spoke to Stearns County, but knowledge of his tip left me with more questions than answers, one of which is how much the other Paynesville police officers knew about Danny Heinrich. I pose this question more out of curiosity than criticism because Heinrich was so unknown to me, and I believe, to the other guys in Paynesville.

Around the same time, the FBI contacted Jared continually, interviewing him, going to his school, having him sit in Heinrich's car, and showing him a lineup. However, this was about a year later and Jared was unable to identify who had kidnapped him. FBI agents actually interviewed Heinrich in February 1990 for Jared's assault but released him without charges. It always seemed too simple, too unfortunate, anticlimactic, perhaps. I know the word "simple" doesn't necessarily convey the meaning I want, but Heinrich said he didn't do it; there wasn't a body, there wasn't enough evidence, and law enforcement officials were forced to release him.

Why Not Duane Hart?

I gave Stearns County my original tip on October 24, 1989. I went to Jerry Wetterling personally in December 1989. Paynesville Police Chief Robert Schmiginsky spoke to Stearns County officials a few weeks later, on January 8, 1990, giving them Danny Heinrich's name as a suspect in the Paynesville attacks. It has always been my assumption that authorities arrested Hart, or at least investigated him because of my tip, since I named him. Stearns County followed up shortly thereafter. Heinrich appeared in a lineup on January 26, 1990.

It's surprising I didn't think of how dissimilar Hart and Chester's modi operandi were, but looking back, maybe it should have been more obvious to me sooner that Hart probably wasn't Chester. I knew and hung around with some of Hart's victims. Hart was visible, out in the open, and people knew him around Paynesville. Particularly interesting, the night at the lake, a couple of kids I knew were hanging around with him, planning to fish with Hart for the opener. Noticing they were talking about partying, I thought Hart got kids drunk or high. Access to beer or weed seemed to me the only reason a kid would hang around with a middle-aged man at that time, and apparently, it's also how he then molested them.

A friend of mine from hockey, whom I'll call Eric, was one of the kids at the lake with Hart that night. Eric seemed comfortable around Hart, unlike me. Hart may have given Eric alcohol or gotten him high, but it was unnerving to me. Feeling dysregulated and agitated physically, I knew that the situation wasn't good. I wanted Eric to come home with us rather than stay with Hart. He didn't. While I never asked Eric or spoke to him about Hart or that evening in particular, I always worried about him—worried that Eric was a victim. Just over a year later, after Jacob's abduction, I called Stearns County and gave them Hart's name as a suspect. I believed it made sense to do so given his propensity for molesting boys and his reputation in Paynesville and the surrounding area.

The point of sharing that experience is that, years later, I learned about how groomers attract victims, but that research was only beginning in the 1980s. As mentioned, authorities arrested Hart in 1990, and in the article about his arrest, they reported that Hart would offer boys presents to lure them and that he once offered a boy $5.00.[8] Dewey Hart certainly groomed his victims. As far as I know, Danny Heinrich merely grabbed and attacked his victims without grooming them. Furthermore, to my knowledge, Danny Heinrich was entirely under the radar for the children in Paynesville.

Nobody I knew or who hung around with me would have ever mentioned Danny Heinrich as a suspect, but everybody knew about Dewey Hart. I had literally never heard of Danny Heinrich as a suspect until his arrest in 2015. This is important for a number of reasons, but primarily because it seems Hart's notoriety permitted Heinrich to run rampant back then, and whether intentional or not, it was almost as though Hart ran interference for Heinrich. This dynamic again begs the questions of how much Paynesville officers knew. What did Chief Schmiginsky know about Heinrich, and what made him a suspect?

Hidden in Plain View

I thought I had no idea who Heinrich was when I lived in Paynesville. Nearly 25 years after he attacked Kirk and the incident at the river, I figured something out. Recalling a woman

---

[8] Douglass. "Charged with Molesting Boys."

with the last name Heinrich who lived two doors down from us at the Black Saucer, I reached out to our former landlord. His mind was clear as a bell—he was over 90 years old at the time I contacted him—and he remembered immediately. He told me the woman's first name, her apartment number, and confirmed that she was Danny Heinrich's mother. I recalled a couple of interactions with her, one in particular during eighth grade, which coincided with the time when Danny Heinrich had started attacking boys.

Walking home from school with my friends Jon and Ann, I saw smoke rising from the part of the town where I lived. Never one to pass up an opportunity for a joke or snide remark, as we got closer and the smoke appeared thicker, I said, "Oh, look, I bet my house is on fire."

My friends' slightly macabre senses of humor prevailed, and laughter erupted. Imagine the horror when we rounded the corner by the church, and I saw the fire trucks in front of the Black Saucer, with firefighters everywhere, including some on the roof cutting a hole to get into the attic.

During this particularly bitter cold stretch of a Minnesota winter—for those in warmer climes, I'm talking about temperatures of 30° below zero—Corrine Heinrich had turned the oven on in her apartment to supplement the heating system. Leaving, she forgot to turn the oven off, and the heat the oven generated was enough to start a smoldering fire in the attic. The fire didn't consume the whole complex, as the fire department contained it to a small area above her apartment.

Knowing most of the people who lived in the apartments, I stopped and talked to her from time to time. I realize now that, at least once during the time he was attacking us, Danny Heinrich was there visiting her when I stopped to chat with her. Corrine Heinrich, her son Danny, and I were standing outside on the balcony. It doesn't occur to me that she even introduced me to him, but he knew me, obviously. Just standing there, looking, I don't think he said a word. He was so much under the radar to me that I didn't think anything of it. During at least some of the time he was attacking kids, I confirmed, too, although many years later, that Heinrich had lived in the Plaza Apartments in Paynesville down the hall from my dad. I don't know for sure if he lived there at the same time as my dad or not, but he clearly did when the attacks were going on. Regardless, while I wouldn't say I met Danny Heinrich, he and I occupied the same space at times. This, I think, underscores how under the radar he was in Paynesville. Danny Heinrich could have easily started watching me early on, at any one of those visits to his mother's apartment, or years earlier when I was visiting my dad.

Seeing Danny Heinrich at his mother's apartment didn't heighten my fear of Chester. Other than being eerily quiet and creepy, Heinrich in no way gave me the sense that he could have been Chester. Chester didn't fit my perception of a child molester. Having lived more years and furthered my education, my understanding is broader today. Back then, especially before he started attacking us, if I even thought about it, I would have thought of child molesters in a stereotypical "Hey kid, do you want some candy?" way. For example, I would have imagined these perpetrators luring kids into a van or using a position of authority as happened in the clergy scandals. Authorities took the tip about Dewey Hart seriously, but I think they tried to find differences between all of our cases and situations while missing, dismissing, or ignoring striking similarities.

When law enforcement turned its attention to Paynesville briefly, things seemed to happen quickly. Arrested, convicted, and sent to jail, authorities moved Hart's case along quickly. The spotlight turned to Heinrich, and the FBI interviewed some of the Paynesville victims; however, the link I thought that seemed to be so clear, so evident, was elusive. Law enforcement backed off from Paynesville completely after Hart's arrest, and this was understandable. After a while, the investigation slowed down. Heinrich had been a suspect in all three cases. Heinrich had cooperated with the FBI and Stearns County; they interviewed him and he turned over property, including tires, tennis shoes, police scanners, boots, and brown caps, among other items. Authorities interviewed Heinrich about Jared's assault in February of 1990 but had no choice but to release him.[9] Later, I'll share and analyze some of the Paynesville connections and angles in more detail, but when I heard about the arrest of a suspect, I was excited.

The excitement quickly turned ice cold when I heard they had released him. I don't remember hearing officials mention Heinrich's name as a suspect, but upon hearing about his release on the news, I remember thinking to myself, "That's it?" Soon

---

[9] Lou Raguse, "Heinrich as Suspect: A Timeline." Last modified September 14, 2016. https://www.kare11.com/article/news/crime/heinrich-as-suspect-a-timeline/314467341

after, it became clear to me that law enforcement was not going to solve the cases anytime soon.

Of course, people were still interested in Jacob's disappearance, but bordering on preposterous, the leads seemed to get steadily crazier. Law enforcement still had to investigate them, at least to rule them out as plausible. By 1991 or so, any momentum in finding Jacob stalled, as far as I could tell. Paynesville had fallen off the radar. There were prayer vigils, continued searches, follow-up news reports, interviews, and the awareness campaign that used the phrase *Jacob's Hope*, even a song written for Jacob. For those of us invested so deeply because of what we experienced, and wanting to bring Chester to justice, the slowdown in the Wetterling investigation left us very discouraged and disappointed. When no arrest resulted from the Paynesville work, I remember a sinking feeling of frustration and loss coming over me. Disheartened, I felt I had put in as much effort as possible to bring attention to the cases, yet the work yielded no arrest. Thinking Chester could get away with his heinous crimes made me terribly angry. By this time, I didn't believe it was Hart. Law enforcement officials knew about Heinrich; we didn't. In my view, they dropped the ball. Before long, Jacob's story no longer dominated the news, and Paynesville once again became a blip on Minnesota Highway 23. Then, as they do, the years passed.

It seemed odd and inconceivable to me how a crime that received so much attention could go unsolved, as Jacob's case did. After authorities left Paynesville without an arrest, I was dumbfounded. Taking some solace in the fact that law enforcement caught and convicted Hart eased the sting of the Paynesville experiences somewhat, but questions persisted. Becoming less dominant in my thoughts over time, the memories associated with the attacks and the damage never completely went away.

PART III
IN THE MEANTIME...FOR
DECADES

CHAPTER 8
27 Years

I was awfully curious to find out why I didn't go insane.
~Abraham Maslow

Nothing Is Stuffed Forever

My friend Matt shared a Sigmund Freud quote: "Unexpressed emotions will never die. They are buried alive and will come forth later in uglier ways." For me, these cases wouldn't go away. With very few exceptions, I never shared with anyone what had really gone on in my life. It's understandable, as those sorts of experiences aren't much of a conversation starter. Imagine it, "So, yeah, back in my hometown, there was this guy who chased boys, groped them at knifepoint, but was never caught. Tell me a little bit about yourself." That which sounded so normal to me, had become commonplace, yet was actually horrific. How did the attacks in Paynesville affect people, myself, and members of law enforcement? What do you do for almost thirty years while waiting for news on the case, longing for answers, justice, and closure? If I was to make it, it became clear I was going to have to move forward, making every cognitive effort to avoid thinking about my experiences. Unfortunately, this avoidance, as opposed to processing, led to my seeking escapes rather than digging in, doing the difficult work, and embarking on the path to healing.

Drinking alcohol for the first time felt truly magical to me. It allowed me to feel settled in my own skin; alcohol made me feel *other than* the person I was. With alcohol, I didn't feel so scared. I didn't worry about Heinrich coming after me from the neighbor's backyard. Having tasted sips of it before and observed how adults' behavior changed when they drank, I knew it would change the way I felt, so I snuck some beers at my great-grandma's estate sale.

Realizing it now, I was already drinking like an alcoholic that first time. Having hidden among some trees, I drank five or so of them in a short enough time that they hit me like a freight train. It isn't that I knew I was going to get drunk, but I knew enough about alcohol that it would change how I felt. That was the secret for me. I needed and sought relief. Stress, chaos, uncertainty—all I knew—alcohol changed all of that, as I didn't have to acknowledge and feel what I felt. The problem is that once I felt that change, I continued to chase it. Alcoholics and addicts often desire to repeat the fun and good times of the first encounter with the chemical(s). Most people don't become problem drinkers, let alone alcoholics. Of those who do, some are fortunate enough to find recovery in a 12-step program or through some other means, but many alcoholics and addicts chase that feeling to any number of institutions, or frequently, to their premature death.

From very early on in life—by high school—I knew alcohol had a grip on me. Seeking relief, I had been smoking cigarettes and dipping snuff at a young age. I started drinking early on in life too. This was culturally acceptable, however, and most people drank alcohol where I grew up. Smoking cigarettes was probably worse than using chewing tobacco or drinking. Over the years, when I've shared that I've never smoked marijuana, people are dubious of that claim. I never tried it because I knew I would become a daily pot smoker, and I would become dependent on whatever else I tried. In hindsight, that was the right decision too, because alcohol caused plenty of problems without adding other substances to the mix.

No amount of alcohol could quench the effects of my experiences. The first time I got drunk was to escape, and I chased that feeling for a very long time. Alcohol changed the way I felt. I earned a master's in Clinical Mental Health, starting classes when the COVID-19 pandemic began. I also have these real-life experiences and anecdotal evidence to make the statement that if you've experienced trauma and feel the need to escape from it with chemicals, hobbies, relationships, or other behaviors, I can attest to how poorly it works in the end. Granted, it typically works for a little while, I believe, but it will eventually stop working. When it does, you'll find yourself alone with your trauma. It stopped working for me, and luckily, I did not continue my search for an external solution to my internal problems.

Longing to feel better, to feel *normal* (whatever that might be), I had sought healing in relationships. Friendships sustained me during some of the worst of my childhood years, but I sought relief in another person, grasping to feel *ok*. In hindsight, I realize therapy would have been immensely helpful. Instead, I married the second person I ever dated, just shy of 22 years old, despite being ill-prepared, immature, and not truly able to relate to people, let alone marry. Despite efforts to find one, there aren't any shortcuts. Unfortunately, I brought all the brokenness from the past into the marriage. It isn't simply that I hadn't worked on anything because I hadn't; in fact, I had not even looked at myself or processed any of my experiences. So filled with anger and resentment, I sought relief and repair from another person, relief that I have since learned simply isn't possible. In addition to drinking, to escape, from about age 19 to 26, I tried many activities to alleviate my anxiety and fear and to fix myself. People who have gone through traumatic experiences may relate to my efforts to seek relief by trying to fill my insatiable void with activities. These included, among others, adult softball, joining a bowling league, obtaining my scuba diving certification, and changing jobs, all of which aimed at making me feel normal. I figured if I could just get *that* or do *it*, I'd be ok in my own skin. None of these efforts worked.

At some point, I—painfully, reluctantly, and angrily—accepted that our cases would go unsolved. Thirteen years and five days after he came running out of the spruce trees to get me, I quit running from Chester. Quitting drinking, I began a journey of healing and recovery. Growing up, maturing (hopefully), and becoming responsible for myself, I stopped blaming Chester or anyone else for where I was in life. Just a few months short of 27 years old, I realized I could have a long time to live and couldn't see myself continuing the way I had been. Traveling a well-worn path, I had experienced trauma, which led to a desire for relief and escape through alcohol, until it stopped working.

The external attempts didn't work for me; I really began to grow and change by attending Alcoholics Anonymous meetings. In AA, I learned a method and language of recovery that emphasized focusing on my own role and part in the process of recovery. This process included making amends for my own mistakes and trying to be helpful to others. AA influenced me early on, piquing my interest in what recovery could do. In early meetings, I heard stories from people who had gone through similar experiences as I had, but they weren't angry. I noticed the AA people were joyful and happy. I longed to be joyful and happy too. People were honestly sharing experiences, speaking openly about tragic topics and events. They shared how they went through these events without drinking; the honesty in most AA meetings is palpable. Early on, I wasn't capable of sharing openly and from the heart; while appealing, I didn't trust anyone enough to do so. As time went on, I learned the value of sharing and gradually opened myself up to deeper friendships and meaningful work in the recovery process. I like to challenge myself continually, to learn and do more; I coupled my interest in recovery with another passion of mine—baseball—and turned more attention to it.

Baseball

This narrative has some unsettling parts, things I wish I hadn't experienced. Reading about some of my experiences probably made people feel uncomfortable. My life has also been fulfilling. Baseball was a constant for me, something consistent in my life. While I wasn't the greatest player, I very much enjoyed playing and appreciated the camaraderie of being on the team. Most likely a function of its history and unique slow pace, baseball, for those who don't know it well, has a culture of one-liners and characters unsurpassed by any other sport.

With encouragement from my high school and American Legion Baseball coaches, I had started umpiring while I was in high school. My coach always said I should go to professional umpire school, but I never did. While I try not to live in regret, I do wonder what that would have been like. Umpiring became a bit of a passion for me over the years, particularly after I stopped drinking. An outlet, too, with hard work and practice, I got to be decent, working my way quickly to high school varsity, American Legion Baseball in summer, college, and adult amateur leagues. Baseball has its own culture, and fortunately for me at that time, drinking was part of it, especially in central Minnesota. Baseball allowed me to escape, drink, and have some long-awaited structure in my life. Besides giving me the opportunity and responsibility to manage the game, it made me feel that I mattered. It was an opportunity to have some say in what was going on in my life and to feel appreciated for working hard and trying to do well, at least later on in my umpiring career. In the beginning, it was less like that and more antagonistic.

For those knowledgeable about baseball, be patient and please forgive me for the following explanation; I don't want to lose any readers with a sports analogy that doesn't make sense to them. Unlike other sports, in baseball, each pitch draws people's attention to the home plate umpire because, unless the batter makes contact with the ball, nothing can happen until the umpire has made a call of ball or strike. The nature of this play creates a tension and feeling of slowness unlike that in other sports. Everyone zeros in on the combination of pitcher, catcher, umpire, and batter. Nothing can happen outside this sphere without the ball, so it's the focus of attention. The umpire has to rule on pitches in or out of the strike zone. Without getting too technical, this is a box-shaped area over home plate roughly between the kneecaps and just below the batter's shoulders. If the pitch enters this area, the batter either swings at the pitch, hitting it or not, or lets it go by, requiring the umpire to call (judge) it a strike or ball. Four ball pitches that aren't strikes permit the batter to get on base. Three strikes, which can be pitches swung at and missed or strikes entering the strike zone called by the umpire, mean the batter is "out."

Homing in on the called strike, I call your attention to how important the umpire's job is in calling the pitches correctly, and to share something I find ironic. If you know baseball, you know this already. Reminded of games you've attended in the past, think about the days you've seen the home plate umpire struggle. The reasons umpires struggle don't matter for the story I'm telling, but few things make an umpire's job more difficult than a pitcher who is having a bad game, followed by a bad catcher. If you're not a baseball fan, I hope I have given you enough of an overview to appreciate what I'm sharing. When a game begins going downhill—recall on each pitch the focus ends up on the home plate umpire—players, coaches, fans, and even announcers form opinions about the umpire's performance. When the pitcher isn't throwing strikes, or the umpire isn't calling them, the batters are less likely to swing at pitches. During times like these in games, some of the greatest one-liners and banter occur.

One favorite insult that players, coaches, and baseball fans direct at a plate umpire is, "Be consistent!" This admonition, screamed from dugouts at umpires across the country, calls into question the umpire's integrity, insults their manhood or womanhood, and generally singles out the umpire, chastising him or her for allegedly not making the correct calls on pitches. When I would hear this accusation yelled at me, I would sometimes smile or chuckle to myself behind my facemask, thinking about how diligently I was working to be consistent. How, above almost anything else in my life, I yearned for consistency and clarity. *Yes, guys, I am trying to be consistent,* I would think. *In fact, you have no idea how much I love consistency and I would never miss a pitch if it were up to me.* It's odd that a lack of consistency and structure manifested itself in baseball. Growing up as I did, I truly empathized with the players' desire for consistency on a level they could hardly understand, even if I had tried to explain it. Although their idea of consistency and mine were in different areas, I always found it interesting how that simple phrase affected me and my efforts in baseball. It motivated me. Despite frequently failing, I strove for consistency in other areas of my life, too, such as being a good father and excelling in school.

Early in my umpiring career, being young and immature—younger, in fact, than many of the players at that time—I had a short fuse and a quick mouth at times, not a good combination for an umpire. For example, at an adult amateur game one summer, a big, right-handed hitter had a 3-0 count and was taking a pitch all the way, trying to force the pitcher to make a mistake, thereby allowing him to walk. As the pitch came in, it was what we call a "gut fastball" on the inside part of the plate. Not the best pitch to hit, it was a borderline strike at best, but with a 3-0 count, close enough. He motioned toward first base as I called the pitch a strike. Turning around, he barked at me, "You called that a strike?!" "Yes, I did," I barked back at him, "and the next two are strikes, too, so you better be swinging." Not at all impressed with my prophecy, he stepped out of the batter's box and said angrily, "How would you like this bat wrapped around your head?" Calling time and dusting off the plate, I went into damage control mode quickly, de-escalating the situation, assuring him that, in fact, I couldn't foresee whether the pitches were strikes until after the pitcher delivered them. He accepted this clarification, luckily, and I learned a valuable lesson about being too mouthy.

What I also realized from this altercation and a few others early on was that my being mouthy and my thin skin had nothing to do with baseball. Players have lipped off to umpires, and vice versa, ever since Abner Doubleday was said to have invented the sport (although he may not have). What mattered for the purposes here is that all I had experienced affected me profoundly and that it was coming out as anger. Baseball and learning to be a good umpire had the power to help me develop some emotional intelligence—to help me stay calm when things were escalating, to work with players and coaches rather than lip off and start throwing people out of the game.

What does baseball have to do with the cases? While living in the St. Cloud area, I lived in a near-constant state of fear for years. I was still stunned and curious about Chester, wondering if he were around, and if law enforcement would ever catch him. Blue spruce trees triggered me. No matter where I went to umpire—especially around Paynesville, Cold Spring, and St. Joseph, MN—I wondered if I was safe, especially at night games. I would scan the stands sometimes between innings or during play stoppages while I was working the bases. I'd wonder if Chester was watching the game, watching me. After the game, we would often have to change out of our uniforms by our vehicles, and I would be on guard. As I got older, I moved past much of my actual fear of physical violence but still always wondered. I'd umpire with others and would question to myself what they knew, if anything, about our cases, and about Jared. I knew everyone knew about Jacob.

Sometimes, feelings of shame would make me feel small and like an impostor—that the *real me* was the scared little boy, not an umpire, especially because umpires have so much responsibility and are such an integral part of the game. Standing on the field, smelling the freshly cut grass, feeling the sunshine and a warm breeze, and seeing the players, fear would strike me, and I'd wonder sometimes if Chester was still around. Umpiring can be so isolating; I'd wonder if the players or even the fans had been through terrible things, and gratitude would come over me that I had survived.

Consistent with other friendships in my life, the camaraderie with other umpires was good for me personally—for friendship with men and for my personal growth. I developed many strong friendships and met a few mentors as well. In the beginning, the assigners would send us out with older umpires to show us the ropes. Many of the men I umpired with over the years taught me about life, not just baseball. They taught me how to handle situations and helped me develop skills I'd use forever. Umpiring taught me so much about people, working with them, handling conflict, and how to be reasonable and to hear people out without conflict.

Teacher

Even though I had literally no idea how I would ever get into college, let alone finish, teaching had always been on my radar while growing up. Teaching appealed to me because of a strong desire to help kids like myself. Getting through college was another story, however; with so few successful academic experiences, I believed my self-esteem was so low that I didn't think I could get into college. I had too much outside negativity to be a focused student. Having been in a state of active emotional trauma and dysregulated for so long, I missed a lot of school. Graduating from high school did not always look very likely. At times, graduating from high school didn't even seem possible. As I mentioned, I always tried to give the appearance that I was like other kids, though.

Like other seniors, I looked at schools, even though I knew intuitively that attending college was not going to happen. On a couple of college visits, I learned that some schools may have accepted me for a semester on a trial basis. Going to college after high school sounded like a good idea, but it didn't happen that way. Having an opportunity to go to a junior college with my friend Matt, I simply didn't know how to make it happen financially. Aside from the emotional issues I was experiencing at the time, I graduated from high school, but I was unlikely mature enough to have done well in college at that point. It was clear to me that academic success depended on experiences and skills I didn't yet possess. I still reeled from my experiences and Chester's impact on my life. It wasn't that I lacked academic ability or interest; I was living in a sort of hell. Something inside me, a very small seed with a sense of desiring to better myself, remained, but it took a while to develop.

After high school, it became clear that working was my only real option. Wanting to get out of my dad's apartment as soon as possible, I began to work full-time after securing a job and moved out about a year after graduation. After working full-time for a couple of years post-high school, I turned 21 and learned that St. Cloud State University accepted any Stearns County resident 21 or older without the usual requisite ACT scores. Encouraged by my girlfriend, I enrolled in one class just to see if I could do it. Earning an A, I realized that finishing college might be possible for me. With a combination of working, taking classes here and there, taking time off from school a couple of times, and changing careers in search of a shortcut, I meandered through college over the course of many years. As I worked various jobs over those years, it seemed I was doing one of two things in alternating fashion.

I would take classes, plodding, pushing myself toward a degree, but then I'd get impatient with my slow progress. I'd use this frustration as an excuse to pursue the second alternative, finding a shortcut. Ultimately, I would return to taking classes. About eight years had passed, and with two years of school left, I took as many courses as I possibly could, including summer and intersession (short, intensive courses), finishing in about a year and a half, relying on my wife's income and what I earned umpiring baseball. Upon completing the degree and licensure program, we moved to southeastern Minnesota, and I began teaching high school. Graduating from college at 31, well past the typical early 20s when many people do, I felt like I had finally caught up a bit. Finishing my degree started to loosen the choking grip trauma had held on me for so long.

PART IV
REVISIT, RESOLVE, SOLVE, REFLECT, AND ADVOCATE

CHAPTER 9
Let's Try This Again

Adversity has the effect of eliciting talents which, in prosperous circumstances, would have lain dormant. ~Horace

I'm prefacing this chapter, as well as the next, by expressing my gratitude for the outcome of the Wetterling investigation, Jared's case, and the Paynesville cases, which led to catching Danny Heinrich. I'm grateful to the team of investigators, particularly Chris Boeckers, FBI Special Agent, and to members of law enforcement, past and present, who persevered, asked the right questions, and were willing to take another look. Their work was crucial in solving these cases, and I am deeply thankful they persisted despite the journey being a long, winding road. The opening of this chapter is a synopsis of how I saw the investigation reopen and how I became involved again. What follows are some of my thoughts and observations about the case, as well as those from at least some of the Paynesville survivors. Admittedly, these views may not align with everyone's narrative and commentary, including various media reports, some law enforcement officials, and others with opinions, of which there are many. In a critique of sorts, I attempt to address some significant gaps in the existing descriptions of these events.

A Phone Call from a Ghost (November 2013)

The exposed brick walls inside the loft apartment in downtown Little Rock, Arkansas, reminded me of the outside wall behind Paynesville Middle School, where I used to shoot baskets. The basket was mounted on the brick wall, and its red, rough brick surface made it possible to get a good grip with your tennis shoes and launch yourself off the wall to dunk the basketball, if you got the timing right. The brick reminded me of Paynesville and brought back many memories.

The loft was my new, albeit temporary, home as my marriage was unwinding and unraveling. In the loneliness, I had plenty of time for reflection, especially when my kids were with their mom. I had lived in the loft for about two months, wondering what would happen, but more importantly, how I had gotten to this point in life. I never saw some of the answers to my past coming the way they did. Sometimes, good things happen when people find their voice. Oftentimes, people find their voice when others aren't ready to hear it, but at other times, people approach with impeccable timing.

I answered the phone.

"Hello."

"Is this Kris Bertelsen? The Kris Bertelsen from Paynesville, MN?"

"Yes, it is. Who is this?"

"Jared Scheierl."

I was flooded with a flush of alternating memories and feelings, including relief, frustration, confusion, anger, and fear, all simultaneously. Just hearing Jared say his name sparked some old frustration I had with how law enforcement handled things. The handling of the Paynesville cases caused disappointment.

Over the years, I had called to speak to someone about the cases and always received similar responses, ultimately implying, "We're law enforcement, and you are not." By the time Jared called me, I had mostly come to peace with the attacks and their effects. After all, I had been in recovery for over 13 years at that point and had worked hard on myself, trying to forgive. Frankly, I had given up any hope that Stearns County would talk to me again about any Paynesville cases and connections to the Wetterling case. To that point, I was not wrong. Decades had passed. Today, I get it. They had wanted to solve the case, too. There was plenty of PTSD and damage experienced by all involved, and there were no breaks in the case.

When Jared called me, it was clear he was on a mission to solve these cases and help the Wetterlings locate their son. Like me, he believed it was impossible to deny that our cases in Paynesville—and his own—were related to Jacob Wetterling's disappearance, and as we now know, murder. Jared learned about the Paynesville cases when Joy Baker, a blogger interested in the Wetterling case, came upon the Paynesville Press articles I've got in this book where Sergeant Drager, pleading, had reached out for the public's help. Without a doubt, I believed Jared when he said he knew nothing about our cases in Paynesville, especially given that he had gone through such terrible trauma himself. Of course, law enforcement had investigated them almost three decades earlier. He had moved to Paynesville to get away from Cold Spring. During that time, his family moved to Paynesville, and much attention had shifted to the Wetterling investigation.

In an astonishing irony, Jared and I went to high school together for a year and a half and knew each other somewhat, though I had no idea who he *really* was. We even had friends in common, boys a little younger than me whom I kept watch over, making sure they had a knife for protection. People went to great lengths—thankfully—to protect his identity. Nobody would expect Jared to move to a new town and ask about whether there had been any violent child molesters or kidnappings in town.

During our first talk on the phone, I found myself feeling the old, lingering, annoying exasperation and frustration. Explaining, somewhat jokingly, to him that he was almost thirty years late to the game and that I didn't believe it was Dewey Hart, I told Jared I would help if I could. We hit it off right away and were on a mission together. Refusing to let go of a possible connection to Paynesville, I had always stood outside the investigation, always on the edge, but metaphorically beating down the door. Now, an ally reached out to me. Jared was passionate and determined. His call and the friendship we developed came just at the right time. Recently divorced—largely related to my experiences and issues stemming from the Heinrich era—Jared and I related well with one another; kindred spirits, we both found someone who understood. Two men who got it. While it brought back the terror, Jared's call reignited my interest in helping find Jacob and got me deeply involved in counseling. As you can imagine, I've always felt like an outsider to the investigation, thinking that law enforcement wouldn't listen, whether that was my perception or reality. Even though the man who had attacked him so long ago was still probably out there, Jared courageously and openly pursued resolution of his case. Going all in one last time to try to solve these cases, he was going on TV, doing interviews, pushing for answers, calling for action, and requesting information from anyone who might have it. Jared refused to back down from anyone who might have said or implied they couldn't do anything.

Through many conversations, amateur sleuthing, support, and interviews, Jared continued enlisting support from whoever and wherever he could. We kept in contact throughout the process—Jared updating me periodically with what he knew as he received information from the FBI. Of course, behind the scenes, law enforcement officials were working hard to bring the perpetrator to justice. Jared asked me to go forward and tell the story, too, as he had done with his. Fear ruled me for quite some time as I agonized over whether to do it. Going public with this type of story when the perpetrator was more than likely still at large was a terrifying prospect. Knowing how important it was to Jared to figure out his attacker's identity and finding Jacob prevailed. With my face blurred on the screen, I did an interview under the pseudonym "Craig." Still frightened because I knew people would recognize me, I finally went ahead with it. Calling for attention and help for the investigation at the end of the segment, Esme Murphy, the reporter, played a huge role in bringing attention to the cause. With extraordinary effort, Jared worked tirelessly on the cases, asking for information from the public, conducting interviews, and calling attention to the unsolved cases. Law enforcement listened and was committed to helping find Jacob's killer.

Arrested

It had been nearly two years in the making from the time Jared called me in 2013—and when the miracle happened, the work paid off in an arrest. The arrest brought answers. All the background information leading to Heinrich's arrest in July of 2015[10] resulted from a fresh look at the cases. The FBI arrested Heinrich, who then faced prison time for child pornography, including nude pictures with middle schoolers' heads pasted onto the photos. This marked the beginning of the next phase for Jared and the Wetterling family: finding Jacob.

The Wetterlings lived all those years not knowing what had happened to Jacob. Now we finally knew that "Chester the Molester," the faceless, nameless attacker who had stalked my friends and me, had a name. The Paynesville victims had lived 30 years not knowing who was terrorizing us, causing tremendous pain and often debilitating fear. Danny Heinrich turned out to be my boogeyman. After getting away from him twice, the terror of his coming after me reverberated through my life, affecting some things even today—for example, the chills I get when people stand right behind me, looking over my shoulder.

Having finally accepted what Heinrich had done to us, and recognizing the shortcomings of the investigation up to that point, I worked diligently to move past all this as best I could. Taking the liberty of speaking for the Paynesville victims, I would say that not knowing the identity of our pursuer made it difficult to accept and move past our experiences. Imagining him coming after me repeatedly, I lived with a feeling of terror

---

[10] Raguse, "Heinrich as Suspect."

because of what he had done to my friends and me. A face and a name, not to mention an arrest and conviction, would have aided the healing process—much sooner, too, especially had it not taken nearly 30 years.

Over the years, several themes and people's own creative narratives have surfaced about what happened to Jacob Wetterling. Some individuals dabbled in truly wild leads, stories, and hypotheses about the case. As I mentioned previously, the case files are voluminous. If you've read this far, you know I have always believed the cases were related.

I don't recall the prosecuting attorneys mentioning the Paynesville victims specifically, but the Paynesville cases were part of the request for the search warrant and affidavit. Heinrich never admitted in court that he was Chester; however, we do have the close DNA match from his hat—the one Kirk grabbed from him in May 1987—along with his own admission to "other victims" in the sentencing. Due to statutes of limitations, authorities didn't charge Heinrich with all of his crimes, including the Paynesville molestations, but prosecutors made it work, so to speak. Furthermore, DNA on the hat from the night he attacked Kirk, Heinrich's own reference to other victims, and our inclusion in the court documents in the case against Heinrich show the importance of the connections to the Paynesville cases in ultimately catching Heinrich.

Solved

A stressful time in life affected me so profoundly that my ultimate objectives in working with Jared included finding Jacob's whereabouts and determining who had assaulted Jared. I always assumed, at a gut level, that the same perpetrator who attacked us in Paynesville might have committed these other crimes. Believing the Paynesville cases were related to the others, I held on, despite a feeling that law enforcement had given up, and that they would probably never solve them. Shockingly and gratefully, I got a chance to find out. This outcome was akin to what I had in mind when I first started speaking to Jared. Statutes of limitations meant that Heinrich's sentence resulted from a plea agreement, but we got answers.

With the information we now have, and with Danny Heinrich incarcerated, I have an opportunity to share perspective on matters I've harbored for a long time—about 35 years as of this writing. Finding strength through grace, I've maintained a balanced approach. I have been outwardly patient with law enforcement over the years after all, they afforded me ample time to practice patience. Not all Paynesville victims who have spoken publicly have held back on their opinions. I understand that. While initially extremely frustrated by what I thought law enforcement should investigate and whom the investigators should speak to, I remained silent.

A letter to the editor and a couple of interviews that only alluded to my frustration were the exceptions. This was not solely my doing. Filled at times with a desire to unleash venom on those investigating the case way back when, yet maintaining an outwardly calm appearance while internally conflicted and frustrated, has taken all the patience I can muster. With Stearns County, in particular, I have tried to be patient. Again, as a teenager, I perceived investigators as showing little interest in the information we had to share, or at least, they did not acknowledge they were checking it out. Showing restraint would probably not have been possible for me had it not been for the example set by Jerry Wetterling—calm and focused, Jerry refused to talk negatively about the case. Over time, I have come to understand the investigation more, but in the following section, I will share some thoughts I have harbored for a long time.

A Paynesville Perspective

I don't need to cast doubt on the investigation or law enforcement officials in the following sections: they have been doing that themselves for thirty years. I'm going to share in order to point out some questions and give people the perspective from a kid who was there. I am not going to criticize anyone for the sake of criticism. In fact, there are good arguments as to why I'm wrong about some of the things I share, and I admit my bias. My point is simply that the feelings I had over the last 30 years or so were what they were, and they affected lives; they mattered.

If you're so inclined, I'd like readers to draw their own conclusions using other sources of information, but please include this one. We lived through these events, and I want to break down a few common beliefs and hypotheses about the cases. Some date from way back when; others are recent arguments about how law enforcement handled the cases in the past and how they ultimately solved them. Again, because I was on the outside of the investigation, this is how I saw it. I'll reiterate that I have looked at the released files, and they are enormous. In each of the three instances that follow, there were discrepancies between what we knew and reported to law enforcement versus what law enforcement and various media reports said publicly. I'm going to go through a few of the common discrepancies that kept coming up over the years. I'll share my perspective, posit a few questions, and conclude the chapter with a "what if" discussion. Before beginning this section and the following chapters, I want to be clear that I'm writing from a place of peace and serenity, filled with gratitude that law enforcement caught Danny Heinrich that Jared received his answer, that the Wetterling family finally got their answer, and were able to find their son. The following simply adds to the conversation, offering a firsthand perspective that too few people know. Frankly, the Paynesville story isn't for outsiders to tell.

The next couple of sections are my outside view, recollection, and observations of what went on in the Wetterling investigation from about 1990 to 2013. My perception was my reality, affecting so many aspects of life; the fact that Chester was still out there and free never left my mind. How could it? Being so integrated with the Wetterling case from the beginning, I felt I was somewhat in the loop and knew what was being done in the investigation. However, in reality, we weren't in the loop. In fairness, I was on the opposite side of the desk from law enforcement, so to speak, so this is how I interpreted what was and wasn't happening. It's not as though the investigators kept us updated or even remained in contact. We couldn't expect them to do so; that would be an unreasonable expectation for many reasons, not the least of which was the fact that we were minors. Furthermore, the case was cold for years. I don't believe this is an armchair quarterback reflection because I was there. I admit I did assume what was (or wasn't) going on behind the scenes. Later on, I'll share what I saw and thought might be helpful at the time of the Wetterling disappearance. I'll spend some time looking back at how investigators might have handled some things differently and perhaps sooner.

Investigators interviewed many of the Paynesville victims. They spoke to enough of us to know what had taken place there. They had enough touch points from various sources that claiming ignorance was not possible, and law enforcement officials did not do so. Some others have, including media. Some victims gave one statement and never heard from law enforcement again. As I have gotten older, I have learned some of the reasoning behind a single statement, versus the possible confusion that can come from more than one. However, the feelings were what they were, as was the anxiety, fear, and doubt.

What I still find strange is how I had to go—or at least felt I had to go—to Jerry Wetterling directly, attempting to force them to consider what we had shared with them. That law enforcement officials didn't contact me after my initial tip was baffling, but again, that was partially a function of my age at the time, and that we in Paynesville had been dealing with this for many years with no arrest. Frustration had already been high from not being able to live as normal kids.

Paynesville Was Not New Information

The Paynesville attacks received reignited attention when Jared began pushing for a cold case review. Jared asked media outlets, particularly Esme Murphy of WCCO-TV in Minneapolis, to help push the cause of solving the cases. Joy Baker came upon the Paynesville Press articles I mentioned earlier. Luckily, enough of us were alive and willing to help in any way we could. Furthermore, when they started back to work on the case, they assembled the right FBI team for the job, without doubt. Before

I continue, let me clarify something and get this out of the way: the notion that the Paynesville attacks were unknown until 2013, or thereabouts, is preposterous. I've heard this, and it makes me feel ill. It minimizes the Paynesville victims, too. I will argue that those saying they were unaware are in denial, chose to ignore the facts, or were so misguided about what they thought was the right path they simply refused to look at the information we gave them. My contact with Stearns County right after Jacob's abduction, my going to Jerry Wetterling in December of 1990, and Paynesville Police Chief Schmiginsky's tip naming Heinrich constitute three separate touchpoints regarding the Paynesville attacks. Moreover, this does not include contact investigators had with other Paynesville victims.

Stearns County investigators were looking into the information I gave them; if not, Jerry did pass the information along to authorities—that's what matters. I've read that investigators received over 80,000 leads.[11] The fact remains that investigators had heard of them more than once. At the very least, they heard from me, then from Chief Schmiginsky, in that order. Different people, myself included, gave them victims' names to interview in Paynesville, and they did interview them. They arrested Duane Hart following my tip. They questioned and arrested

[11] David Unze. "DNA Cracked Wetterling Case." *The St. Cloud Times*, September 23, 2016. https://www.sctimes.com/story/news/local/2016/09/23/dna-cracked-wetterling-case/90849308/
[12] Unze, "DNA Cracked Wetterling Case."

Danny Heinrich too, who, 27 years later, eventually confessed to the crime. Those comments may come off sounding like a tacit indictment of the investigators' work, which is frankly unwarranted.

Following Up on Every Lead

Officials stated that they thoroughly investigated every lead. Stearns County officials have made this public. It makes me wonder if that's a reason they didn't connect Paynesville and Cold Spring. They scaled the investigation up quickly, broadly in scope and geography. Perhaps Paynesville seemed too distant as well. Sheriff John Sanner asserted that they had circumstantial evidence against Heinrich but an otherwise weak case.[12] His successor publicly contradicted the previous handling of the Wetterling investigation, but all of this is for you to think about and decide.

I have had mixed experiences with my interactions with various people involved in the cases. I have never spoken to then Sheriff John Sanner, but I have contacted others. Janelle Kendall, Stearns County Attorney, was extremely helpful in explaining the legal aspects in detail to me as they pertained to Heinrich. Other times, I felt nothing short of exasperated.

I had contacted the lead Stearns County investigator on the Wetterling case in late 2013 or early 2014. I explained who I

---

[12] Unze, "DNA Cracked Wetterling Case."

was, provided the background about what we experienced in Paynesville, and, again, shared the possible connections to all three cases and suggested others who might have information. In that conversation, I specifically mentioned the hat Kirk grabbed from Heinrich in May 1987. She confirmed they still had it, but she wasn't forthcoming about the investigation, or any possible connections to Paynesville. The conversation gave me an off-limits feeling. Frustrated, but not surprised, I felt the need to persist, saying something like, "You have the hat; now go on and investigate it with DNA analysis." I didn't say anything. I refrained from being unkind, believing this investigation had likely taken its toll on her, her staff, and many others in her circle, just as it had on mine. She matter-of-factly delivered what I'd consider a programmed, pat, rote response that there was nothing to see here. In effect, she said, "Move along, we've got this." Looking back, I guess this was understandable. What had started for me as excitement with a reinvigorated desire to help ended with what I felt was a blow-off, feeling law enforcement was ignoring me. Here again, I can see how one can get to the point of having this kind of response, literally having to have a response ready. It had to get old dealing with all that went along with such a huge case.

Nevertheless, our conversation triggered old feelings I'd had during the investigation. Stearns County always evoked the reaction and feeling that I was an annoying dog trying to get my owner's attention or the unpopular kid on the playground excluded from kickball, hoping to be allowed to play. In various media appearances, Sheriff Sanner maintained that the team had investigated every lead. Fair enough. With the exception of the very first statement I gave them, filled with hope that we might help find Jacob, I have always felt like one of those so-called meddling kids in a "Scooby-Doo" cartoon episode, unable to get through to law enforcement. These feelings could very well have been brought on by my own expectations. From this side of the desk, it gives me pause. I do understand that law enforcement officials had thousands of leads and tips to comb through, but I've felt the following are worth consideration and shed light on the frustration on the part of some of the Paynesville victims and Jared.

The FBI and Stearns County had our original statements from Heinrich's attacks in Paynesville. Before the FBI arrested Heinrich in 2015[13], I contacted them. Chris Boeckers, an agent on the team that ultimately helped solve the case, told me he didn't need any additional information; he had everything from back in 1986 to 1989. I respect this and understand that the FBI and Stearns County investigators would want to avoid group-think by not having all the Paynesville victims together to discuss the investigation 30 years after the events. It comes as no surprise to me that Boeckers and the team solved the case with the original statements and evidence, adding the DNA information. I had always believed the cases were solvable with the information investigators had, but that had not happened. I could have been wrong. Back in early 1990, I believe, the FBI conducted a blitz in Paynesville and sent agents to interview victims

---

[13] Raguse, "Heinrich as Suspect."

and community members. The cases were front and center, but they just didn't result in finding Jacob.

We Thought It Was Hart

Tragically, thinking Hart was the perpetrator is an understandable position and a plausible argument. I can't blame officials if they believed it. Granted, it was right to suspect Hart, and law enforcement officials were right to check him out for many reasons. Personally, I suspected him too, until I later learned more about grooming versus grabbing. I named him in my original tip. Many people considered Hart *the* suspect in the Paynesville cases. Hart's 1990 arrest conceivably caused the investigators to stop focusing on Paynesville, unfortunately. This outcome is quite likely, given his history. Furthermore, the Paynesville attacks seemed to stop after Hart's arrest. While possibly a coincidence, this could very well have been the reason for officials to stop looking in Paynesville. It would make sense to think there was nothing more worth investigating there. We can assume, now, the attacks stopped not because officials arrested Hart, but because Heinrich, perhaps feeling the heat in Paynesville, had moved on to Cold Spring and then St. Joseph. Perhaps this was an unfortunate coincidence, leading law enforcement to conclude Hart was responsible for everything in Paynesville.

The part of this case I find so unbelievable is that, although I have been somewhat critical of law enforcement's actions—assuming, perhaps, there were two, three, or even more separate pedophiles in the area committing these crimes—the fact is there were two in the little burgh of Paynesville. Again, law enforcement deserves the benefit of the doubt on this point. I assume it is, in fact, exceedingly rare to find two pedophiles of such notoriety in a small town like Paynesville. Having said that, it is important to note that Hart apparently reported information about Heinrich to law enforcement. According to Hart, Heinrich told him that he had a ninja suit and had asked Hart how to get rid of a body. I believe law enforcement did not follow up on this information, presumably because they did not believe Hart to be a credible source of information.

There was, however, an important difference between Hart and Heinrich, and maybe it was the reason Heinrich was under the radar. Buying presents, alcohol, and drugs, or paying kids, Hart was primarily a groomer. In Paynesville, the perpetrator (Heinrich) attacked victims violently, using guerrilla tactics. Law enforcement knew about both of these suspects but perhaps not as much about Heinrich. In the Paynesville attacks, Jared's assault, and Jacob's disappearance there was no luring per se, just the threat or use of violence to get victims to comply. Heinrich asked Jared for directions, but that was all—threatening him and intimidating him to get into the car. With Jacob, the threat of violence—saying he would shoot if anyone turned around— is inconsistent with grooming, but very much like the threatening statements he made to Paynesville victims. I understand perpetrators tend to fall along the lines of grooming or grabbing their victims. There was not as much information about grooming molestations versus strangers accosting boys back then.

Using clergy abuse as a comparison, perpetrators generally used their positions of authority and respect to build relationships with children. What seemed acceptable in the beginning was, in reality, perverted and manipulative. Dewey Hart acted similarly. People knew Hart, and he used incentives to attract children. This clearly was not the case with Heinrich in any of the crimes he committed in Paynesville, and, to my knowledge, no one has since come forward to say Heinrich groomed them. Early on, around the time of my tip, law enforcement focused on Heinrich, but the pieces did not come together at that time.

The Cases Aren't Related

After Heinrich abducted Jacob and I heard about what happened to Jared, I couldn't help wanting to ask the investigators, "Do you really think there are three different perpetrators doing these terrible things to boys?" There have been various perspectives in news reports over the years. I think it's safe to say law enforcement was hot and cold on Hart and Heinrich. It always seemed officials came *that close* to catching Heinrich. There also seem to have been a number of law enforcement officials who thought the crimes committed against Jared and Jacob were by the same person. Some stopped short of saying the Paynesville attacks were connected to Jared and Jacob because of key differences. However, it's certainly worth noting that the kids were all around the same age and within 25 miles of each other. The crimes took place in a very similar manner, with some differences. The perpetrator said similar things to the victims. For example, he made the same threats to them, saying such things as not to turn or he'd shoot, and the like. While there are some differences between the three cases, the similarities are glaring, and I believe, nearly impossible to refute.

The differences included that in Jared and Jacob's cases, he kidnapped the victims, whereas in Paynesville, he didn't. The threat or use of violence is consistent. The other elements are eerily similar and terrifyingly so to someone who was there. The similarities weaken the position that the cases are unrelated. From what I experienced, I would never have suggested there was no relationship between the crimes, or that multiple predators committed these crimes. I would never consider the latter a viable prospect, and because it doesn't make much sense, I'm not spending much time on it.

Inter-and Intra-Agency Communication

Inter-agency communication, which involved separate contact points with Stearns County and the FBI, led to the investigation of the Paynesville incidents. While it is possible—and there are other examples like the 9/11 terrorist attacks intelligence—to assume poor communication, it simply isn't true. Considering the implications of such poor communication seems absurd. It would mean that the FBI sent agents to Paynesville to interview victims of similar crimes but never reported the findings to their superiors. Alternatively, it would suggest that the agents who went there had no idea why their superiors sent them to interview these children. That notion is comical. Moreover, could two people, including a chief of police in a municipality within the county where the crimes took place, contact an agency at least three separate times and still somehow claim they had never heard of the information? Doubtful. How negligent would an agency have to be to ignore a tip from a chief of police? That entire scenario is implausible, and it did not happen that way. The FBI sent agents to Paynesville to interview children and adults. The steps taken in the investigation demonstrate that comments about not knowing information and not following up are inconsistent and untrue. For instance, the FBI arrested Heinrich the first time in 1990. The agencies did communicate and did follow through on the leads from Paynesville, Cold Spring, and elsewhere. These efforts, unfortunately, did not culminate in finding Jacob or securing a conviction.

Chester's Hat and DNA Evidence

Previously, I mentioned that Kirk got Chester's hat, which came off in the scuffle with him in 1987. It was a long-billed, dark hat, possibly dark blue. At that time, there were versions of this type of hat, often with phrases screen-printed on them, including sexual innuendos such as "Mine's Longer Than Yours." You may remember or have seen them. They were mesh in the back and size-adjustable with the pull-apart plastic parts. Paynesville Police Department officers went around town showing the hat and asking people if they had ever seen anyone wearing it. I'm not trained in police work, so I don't know what the protocols were back then or would be today for handling something like this, but I remember thinking it was an odd way of trying to catch a suspect. I remember Kirk and me questioning the decision to show the hat to people in town, as we believed it would tip off Chester. Instead, at that time, as a 14-year-old boy, I wanted them to try a sting operation or something more adventurous than asking people around town about the hat. I wondered, "Why not try to set him up with a decoy?" While I realized they weren't going to do that, I wanted to trust that they were doing something. Besides, it seemed obvious if they were showing everyone the hat around town, Chester would surely change his outfit to throw the authorities off track. Kirk was upset when he heard the police were showing it to people, thinking there must be some other way.

A recurring theme throughout the saga and in reports from law enforcement of Danny Heinrich's arrest and sentencing was how DNA was *the* break in the case, and indeed it was. Paraphrasing, Sheriff Sanner said that DNA evidence provided authorities with new leads and information to act on in the case of Jacob Wetterling's abduction and possible murder.[14] Giving law enforcement the benefit of the doubt, they did find new DNA on Jared's clothing when they reanalyzed it with new technology in 2012. They matched this up with the police reports and statements from the 1980s because, I would argue, Chris Boeckers and the team were so diligent and thorough. However, I think it's important to note and discuss a caveat or two. I believe DNA solved the case, but it may not be entirely complete, or at the very least, it raises some questions.

With all due respect, while I'm not a scientist, I believe accuracy in DNA testing was available before 2012. DNA analysis became more and more reliable in the late 1990s. Just a couple years after Jacob's disappearance, for example, prosecutors brought DNA up in the O.J. Simpson trial, and within a couple of years of that, DNA was mainstream and widely accepted, right? It raises the question of why it took more than 20 years to conduct DNA analysis. Why didn't the thought occur to anyone to look at Jared's clothing articles, or the fibers collected in 1990 from Heinrich's car, and run some tests on them in, perhaps,

---

[14] Unze, "DNA Cracked Wetterling Case."

about 2000, 2004, when Sheriff Sanner took office, or maybe 2007? Pick a year, but you get my point. Heinrich had been a suspect for years. If law enforcement took time to build a strong enough case to excavate a neighbor's place (which I'll discuss shortly), there doesn't seem to be a reason to wait so long to analyze the DNA. I concede, maybe it was technology or knowing where to look and what to look for. It seems too long to me because Heinrich was free this entire time. The Bureau of Criminal Apprehension ran DNA from Heinrich's hat in 2014.[15] Previously, I mentioned I had contacted the lead investigator in 2013 or 2014. I'm not suggesting I forced law enforcement officials' hand, but the timing was conspicuous. Jared was pushing Stearns County hard during this time, too, wanting them to move on the cases. I would argue that Jared's tenacity helped make it happen. It wasn't on law enforcement's radar, or at least the investigation seemed to have run out of gas. Despite all that time passing, handling, and contamination, the test results ruled out 80.5% of the world as the hat's owner.

What If? How Paynesville Might Have Helped Sooner

I'll preface this section by saying that some of the following are my own long-held ideas about the investigation. There are some good reasons for disagreeing with me, but I have thought

---

[15] Raguse, "Heinrich as Suspect."

about them for so many years, I want to share them. I'll comment briefly on the drawbacks of each. Admittedly, the following is speculative, but I'll pose the question: What would it have hurt to complete the following three tasks? They include a thorough search of Paynesville, a lineup of the same suspects that Jared saw for the Paynesville victims, and a voice lineup, also including the Paynesville victims. I thought these three additional actions by law enforcement could have been helpful and at least had some potential to help solve the case sooner. Members of law enforcement would most likely disagree with my call for a voice lineup, saying they aren't effective. They may very well be right, but it was one I always thought might work because of how the other victims in Paynesville described his voice.

I always thought they would likely have yielded some results earlier, such as eliminating suspects. Aside from speaking to the Paynesville Police Department and other victims, there are other areas, and I think the Misfits would agree, that might have shifted momentum and hurried the case to a conclusion. These may have changed the outcome following Heinrich's arrest the first time. I'll go through three parts where I believe consulting the Paynesville victims could have been helpful but weren't. The second and third of these have been the source of frustration and anger for some victims for many years. As you read through the following, please keep in mind that I could be wrong.

Scour Paynesville

I don't suggest law enforcement didn't look at Paynesville at all because we know they did. Officials searched other areas extensively but not Paynesville. Further, when Sergeant Drager and Chief Schmiginsky were still alive, it may have been beneficial for Wetterling investigators to go back to Paynesville and speak to them. I hope they did, but I don't know. Early on in the investigation, I don't believe authorities ever thoroughly searched the Paynesville area. The reason they didn't in late 1989 and early 1990 was the harsh winter weather. That makes sense, but it seems they should have come back and canvassed the area extensively. After all, Heinrich led authorities to Jacob's body right outside town. Had there been no reason to go there, it would make sense, but Heinrich and Hart were two huge reasons to search the area, I believe. At the time, the search for Jacob was, I believe, the largest of its kind in Minnesota and may have been the largest ever in the country. Experts would likely push back on my idea of searching Paynesville, and there are reasons for that, but the fact is they did search many areas, and in my view, had good reason to check Paynesville. I know searches aren't easy as people get fatigued, and searches require many resources, but I would offer that a search of Paynesville might have made sense. Officials put forth time, energy, and resources to search other areas; I'm not sure why they'd rule out Paynesville.

Do Lineup with the Paynesville Victims

Conducting a lineup with individuals from each of the Paynesville cases always made sense to me, but law enforcement never did it. They had their reasons, which I will detail shortly. Officials had the victims' statements because the FBI had been to Paynesville, and Stearns County had several touchpoints that I've previously mentioned. Law enforcement used lineups frequently, but I think this is changing. Conducting a lineup would have been consistent with what officials did during other investigations at the time. It would have been easy for law enforcement to conduct another one and have the Paynesville victims look at the same lineup Jared did. I always thought, "What would it have hurt?" Set up the lineup, have the Paynesville victims come in individually and look at the suspects, taking notes to compare after they left the room. Had the Paynesville victims identified Heinrich several times, would that have turned the tide in the investigation? Possibly. Clearly, it would have given officials more to go on, perhaps more reasons to investigate further and to continue focusing on, building a stronger case against, and questioning Heinrich.

The answer to my own question, "What would it have hurt?" is complex. As an adult, I understand why law enforcement did not allow a group of minors to participate in a lineup when the perpetrator was wearing a mask in most, if not all, of the incidents. Lineups are not that effective either. Nevertheless, the feelings I had that law enforcement should have conducted a lineup were consistently intense.

Hear Heinrich's Voice

The only time I ever heard Danny Heinrich speak was at his sentencing, but people's knowledge and recall of his distinct voice preceded him. A constant common denominator: victims often described the suspect's raspy voice, a low whisper. As a kid, I remember the victims talking about it—they all said it; it's in the police reports I've seen, too. One victim stated in the report that he might recognize the voice. Investigators could have recorded voice samples for the Paynesville victims who heard him speak and played the samples for them in or out of a lineup setting. Back during the time when Chester was coming after us, several of the victims pointedly commented on his voice, making it sound as if hearing him speak was unmistakable—this was consistent with other accounts, too. Even while the attacks were ongoing, the voice seemed like a consistent attribute. A voice lineup seemed like such a simple thing to do: have each suspect say one of the lines victims reported hearing when the perpetrator attacked them. Like the lineup, compare notes and see what actions to take next. I understand that voice lineups, like regular ones, aren't perfect, and there were any number of issues with conducting one with minors. It has made me wonder how and why they followed some leads so much and some not. Law enforcement officials did not do the lineups I mentioned; for example, yet Stearns County spent years—and one can only speculate on how many taxpayers' dollars and work hours—building a case against a man who had nothing to do with any of them.

Why Follow *That* Guy?

Sitting at my desk in my classroom at St. Charles High School in 2010, I read a news article or watched a video clip online of how Stearns County Sheriff John Sanner was following up about a possible lead in the Jacob Wetterling abduction case. As I recall, the article billed it as new information in the case. Sheriff Sanner, who took office in 2004, was someone I had never talked to. I couldn't believe my eyes. The report underscored how the new information led to the excavation of Dan Rassier's place, located down the road from the Wetterlings, right near the spot from where Heinrich took Jacob. Sheriff Sanner referred to Rassier as "a person of interest" in the Jacob Wetterling investigation. I don't like the moniker. A person of interest, as far as I could ever tell, really meant someone about to have his or her life scrutinized, ripped apart, and changed permanently and unimaginably, while never being called a suspect. What a euphemism. The scene was surreal, and honestly, laughable to me.

In my view, they hadn't done all they could have in our cases and never ruled out the Paynesville area. Yet, despite a lack of similar physical characteristics, here they were, excavating a man's property who did not fit the suspect's description in stature or voice. Imagining Heinrich and Rassier standing together generates an absurd example of two people who look nothing alike, which, in fact, they do not. Over the top, but funny, I thought of Danny DeVito and Arnold Schwarzenegger in the movie *Twins*. I struggled to see the point and reconcile Stearns County's choice to follow Rassier all those years but refuse to look into the connections I pointed out to them. Jared Scheierl has shared with me that he told law enforcement that Mr. Rassier was not the person who assaulted him. Why would they push forward for years investigating Rassier? The only plausible explanation for that would be the belief that the crimes were unrelated, although that argument never made sense to me. To me, it would have made more sense to go to the three things I mentioned previously. If not helpful, they still would have been simpler—and perhaps cheaper—than excavating the Rassier place, and likely much more productive.

Law enforcement found nothing on Rassier's place. Of course, people understand that law enforcement naming him a "person of interest" in such a heinous crime, known nationally, did collateral damage to his reputation, which, to my knowledge, no one from Stearns County took action to correct on Rassier's behalf. They called the dogs off Rassier when Heinrich confessed, but when asked about investigating Rassier, Sheriff Sanner, not surprisingly, defended his actions completely. Citing information contained in the search warrants, the fact that Rassier was by himself the night of the abduction, and the manner in which Rassier answered questions, Sheriff Sanner said that, in fact, he would do the same thing over again if he had to do so. "Shame on us if we don't do what we did," Sheriff Sanner said.[16]

Frustration Containment

When I read the article in which Sheriff Sanner made these comments, it struck a nerve. The writer quoted me in that article as well, so I am familiar with it. I am not writing from a place of anger. While some of the Paynesville survivors were highly critical, both in public and in private, including me at times, I have tried to temper and moderate what I have said about the investigation to the media. I have tried to be understanding of where law enforcement was coming from. I am using this section to explain how and why I tried to do that. At the end of the day,

---

[16] Unze, "DNA Cracked Wetterling Case."

Danny Heinrich is the person who caused all the trauma, hurt, and PTSD associated with the cases. I am not even angry with Heinrich. There is a story in his life. It took a long time for me to get to that place, but there is no point in living in the past or for me to eviscerate people in the present.

In interviews in newspapers and on TV, journalists have asked about my feelings toward law enforcement. Prior to Heinrich's arrest, there were no answers for any of the cases. They hadn't found Jacob, there were no answers for Jared, and certainly no arrest in the Paynesville attacks. From a practical perspective, then, it didn't make sense to lambast the authorities who were supposed to be working on the cases. Learning from the example the Wetterlings set, I tried to see the work law enforcement was doing, to trust, and to leave the outcome to God. Refraining from expressing frustration and anger took discipline, but I attempted to do that. As I said above, I will return to this topic later, but it is worthwhile to note that I have had some feelings of contempt for the Stearns County Sheriff's Office over the years. Those feelings were not because of mistakes, misgivings, or failings, but rather my perception of their lack of response and a general aura that reflected what I felt was an attitude suggesting, "You do not know what you're talking about" and "We are right." With some notable exceptions, the message and theme I've felt from Stearns County is one of "You don't matter." I admit that I likely filled in some blanks where officials didn't intend any malice. It helps to remember that we all grew up with these crimes unsolved, and that was incredibly unnerving and frustrating to live through. Naturally, law enforcement was an easy target for frustration.

It had gotten to the point—through Jared's tenacity and per-severance—that Stearns County accepted he wasn't going away. Further, it became increasingly difficult to ignore the connections to Paynesville, culminating in Heinrich's sentencing.

The Press Conference 2016

For almost 30 years, I have heard how hard law enforcement tried to solve the Wetterling abduction case, which I think is true. Why not? There's no reason to doubt it. There were people involved in all aspects of the case who were well intentioned and worked hard to bring Heinrich to justice. They didn't get the results, but they worked hard. In my mind, I can hear Sheriff Sanner say that this is an ongoing investigation. For people wondering about the whereabouts of their son, or others whose little boy was abducted, sexually assaulted, and left to run home in the dead of a Minnesota winter, working hard just fell short. I was never concerned whether the investigators were working hard or not; I knew they were. That wasn't the point. I questioned what they were not working on and what they chose instead. The Rassier farm dig is a case in point. It seemed they got on a cold lead, probably many, and followed the wrong path(s), and kept going, in Rassier's situation, persistently, for years. How does that happen while they hadn't analyzed DNA on a known person of interest with so many elements in common with all the crimes and an uncanny physical likeness? Despite the frustration I felt, I'm grateful the FBI, Sheriff Sanner, and everyone else finally solved the cases.

The image seared deeply and permanently into my mind's eye as I watched and now recall and picture the press conference announcement when Danny Heinrich confessed. Heinrich admitted to Jared's assault and to abducting, assaulting, and murdering Jacob. I lived in Arkansas at the time of the press conference, so I watched from far away. The leader and survivor, Jared Scheierl, was at the mic. Behind him were Deputy Daniels and Sheriff John Sanner, along with other officials, including the federal prosecuting attorney and FBI officials.

The Paynesville victims didn't feel like they mattered to law enforcement. Granted, the perpetrator didn't kidnap or kill any of us, but it is hard to describe how life changed because of what Heinrich put some of the Paynesville victims through with his crimes. Chris Boeckers and Lauren Schmitz from the FBI communicated with the Paynesville victims, though.

Patty Wetterling spoke—poised, classy, grateful for answers; over the years, she became the consummate voice for children. She has not openly criticized the investigation, as far as I have ever heard, during all these years. Jerry, too, has been supportive of law enforcement, positive and hopeful. In a television interview with Jerry right before the sentencing, I was impressed with his ability to stick to the topic and not slide into criticism of law enforcement, even though it would have been easy to do so. I have tremendous respect for the Wetterling family.

While I am very grateful that Heinrich confessed to Jared's assault and Jacob's murder, and that they were finally able to locate Jacob's remains, the press conference was a stressful, triggering event for me, difficult to watch but impossible to turn off. It was truly a stomach-turning situation. Clearly, finding Jacob was the objective of utmost importance. I watched the press conference with its brief speeches. Excitement, anticipation, and disbelief filled me at his confession. After all those years, I never expected a resolution of any kind. A sinking feeling started to set in as I watched. The press conference focused mostly on the deal the attorneys struck with the defense and how well the teams worked to get this done. The attorneys had nothing to do with the actual investigation and had to work within the confines of the law, including the statute of limitations for each crime.

When Sheriff John Sanner spoke, I wondered if he would discuss Paynesville and the victims there. I was not necessarily surprised when he remained silent on the subject. We were included in the complaint against Heinrich. I waited anxiously to hear acknowledgment of the Paynesville victims and our contribution to the investigation. They did not discuss our role, but there is no denying its importance. The Paynesville cases are a major component of the search warrant and affidavit. The FBI contacted us and said we were pivotal to the investigation. To acknowledge us might have seemed, to them, an admission that they had missed something, but I am not sure. Perhaps he could not do it for legal reasons, but the Paynesville guys' roles behind the scenes were vital. It is unbelievable how these events played out and how some players have been involved from the very beginning. Having taken Kirk's first statement as a Paynesville Police Officer, Deputy Daniels stood behind Jared Scheierl. Daniels, who knew and dealt with Heinrich, went on to work as a Stearns County Deputy Sheriff, and retired.

We got answers, but I stop short of saying we have closure. I'm not a fan of the word when used in instances like this. I won't speak for the Wetterling family, Jared, or any of the other Paynesville victims on that point. Personally, I don't use the word "closure" and never will. The permanence implied by that word does not match the constant presence these events have in me. There are surely lasting effects for my friends and for Heinrich's other victims.

CHAPTER 10
What We Always Thought
Was True

Clouds and darkness surround us, yet Heaven is just, and the day of triumph will surely come, when justice and truth will be vindicated. ~Mary Todd Lincoln

W hether perceived or actual, many of us in Paynesville felt nobody wanted to hear our story. We deduced this from the actions we believed law enforcement took or did not take. Inaction seemed to demonstrate it, although we had no access to behind-the-scenes information. From the time I gave the tip so long ago, it felt as if denial went into full effect. Many of us felt law enforcement officials did not want to hear us. The fact is, law enforcement did listen. They arrested Hart, after all. They arrested Heinrich in 1990. There was no discovery of what happened to us in Paynesville; law enforcement had done their jobs. In 2013, Jared knocked on doors, trying to draw attention to his case and ours. After nearly 30 years, the Paynesville survivors likely say, "I told you so." Aside from Bill Drager and a few others in Paynesville, few people really validated what the Paynesville victims experienced. Admittedly, they were not able to charge Heinrich with those crimes, but the result was enough to create some peace of mind for many people.

Meddling Kids

I know it must be difficult to work reactively, as law enforcement officers do, especially in rare cases like the stranger abductions of children. I can't imagine receiving a phone call that a child has been taken by a stranger and heading to the scene with nothing to go on. The Paynesville narrative matters, however, and I feel I've finally gotten the chance to share this perspective. I've used this book as a platform for pointing out some things I've been thinking for decades. I'm not resentful about anything we experienced, and I'm grateful to Agent Boeckers and the team for solving the case. I pray for the same for the other Paynesville victims, although I know some still struggle. There have been times of despair and disappointment over the years, but hard work proved effective and successful for me in reaching acceptance. Having said that, I find it important to address some lingering feelings many of us grappled with for three-fourths of our lives.

Processing

I'll preface this section with a refresher. By November 2016, we had learned that Danny Heinrich, who had committed all the crimes I discussed, had been sentenced and was in prison. Heinrich had escalated from his start in Paynesville, where he had attacked and groped unsuspecting boys. There were eight documented attacks in Paynesville, and possibly others, occurring prior to Jared's kidnapping and assault and Jacob's kidnapping, assault, and murder. Given that Heinrich took Jacob's life, it would take no wisdom or insight whatsoever to suggest, "It could have been worse for the guys in Paynesville." But Heinrich's abuse in Paynesville and assault on Jared Scheierl scarred many people. From the attacks of which I know some details, I can say confidently, albeit conservatively, that Heinrich's attacks directly affected a minimum of fourteen individuals.

Using 1988 as a starting point (roughly the midpoint of his Paynesville attacks), these victims have been dealing with the effects of terror and loss on some level for over 400 years, collectively. This, of course, doesn't include the victims' family members, spouses, ex-spouses, or children. In the final part of the book, I'll discuss the economics of trauma a little more, but for now, here is a list of the costs of his actions. It matters. What losses—emotional, psychological, and financial—did Heinrich cause? Heinrich went on from his Paynesville attacks to kidnap and sexually assault Jared, then kidnap and murder Jacob Wetterling.

Investigators finally solved the case with DNA analysis and Heinrich's confession to Jared's assault and Jacob's murder. Heinrich led authorities to Jacob's remains located just outside Paynesville on a dairy farm along the Crow River, not far from where we Misfits hung around. Despite numerous terroristic threats, a minimum of ten sexual assaults or attempts, two kidnappings, and a murder, Heinrich had been living in the free world. For nearly 30 years, Danny Heinrich had been free. Although we waited for all those years for Jacob to come home, we now know Heinrich murdered him right away. His other victims spent years wondering, fearing him, and later, fearing for their own children; thus, on some level, many of Heinrich's victims were never truly free.

I'd like to pause, though, and consider things from a bird's-eye view because this unbelievable series of crimes is replete with considerations and questions. The case had been unsolved for decades. Then, some of the victims themselves reignited an investigation out of frustration and anger that there had been no resolution. Conceding they needed to look at it again, law enforcement opened a cold case review. Agent Boeckers and the team meticulously pieced the entire story together, accomplishing what seemed impossible, finally solving it. Utilizing the old information, along with DNA, the team did it. Heinrich's crimes created a wake with people permanently affected.

I'll remind you of the setting and scene at the time in Paynesville. We were kids—11, 12, 13, 14 years old—our friend group was picked apart over the course of two years by a violent, knife-wielding molester terrorizing our town, ultimately changing the trajectory of people's lives, mostly for the worst, at least at the time and at the beginning. I've already shared about the connections between trauma and addiction as seen in my own story. Even as kids, we worked tirelessly to support the investigation. Investigators grilled and interrogated Jared multiple times over details and minutiae, which drove him to the point of a near breakdown, to the point his family moved from Cold Spring to Paynesville. Perhaps at that time, a stronger case against Heinrich was possible by talking to Paynesville victims or taking additional actions. Again, I'd go back to a search, lineup, or voice lineup with the Paynesville victims. I realize law enforcement officials reading this might be cringing. My point is that processing and healing isn't as simple as letting bygones be bygones. We deeply invested ourselves in the cases and the outcome, hoped for the best yet expected the worst. When Heinrich appeared in court, it was, in some ways, the beginning of the process, not the end. I saw Heinrich for the first time outside the shadows, in daylight, in court.

The Public Stance

It might have been all about optics. Sheriff Sanner took office well after Heinrich abducted Jacob Wetterling. He assumed the role of sheriff in 2004. From what I've seen, Sheriff Sanner and his administration have defended themselves and their predecessor's work categorically. That's his job, but over the years, in various sources, I've heard Sheriff Sanner say that they would not change anything about the investigation. I find it hard to believe but understand why he takes that stance. Sheriff Sanner understandably chose his words to avoid any missteps and took a position that they wouldn't have changed anything about the investigation. I think this stance caused more suspicion than acknowledging possible gaps in the investigation would have. Peculiarly, when it came to investigating Mr. Rassier, at one point, Sheriff Sanner stated, "Shame on them if they don't pursue the case against Mr. Rassier." The juxtaposition of pursuing Rassier but not going back to Paynesville until seemingly pressured to do so just looks odd to me. I do acknowledge the burden law enforcement has to investigate tips that may not have merit, but there was at least strong circumstantial evidence in Paynesville—evidence that, coupled with the major findings in DNA analysis, solved the case. I believe it's acceptable to acknowledge things you would have liked to have done differently and not lose credibility with the public. It's difficult to say that when I haven't walked in someone else's shoes, but we waited almost 30 years for answers to this case. I'm not sure exactly what I'd suggest officials might have said or done differently, but I believe some transparency would have gone far and done a lot to rebuild trust. It would have reestablished some of the lost social capital, particularly as it pertained to the Paynesville victims and the Rassier investigation.

Empathy

Lauren Schmitz, FBI Victim Specialist, helped the victims, who wanted it, obtain counseling and worked to provide all relevant information regarding Heinrich's sentencing. Even after the case and sentencing, Boeckers took phone calls and texts and made himself available when we needed to process, as did Schmitz. I mentioned previously how Janelle Kendall, Stearns County Attorney, worked to provide understanding of the legal aspects of the cases. There were many people, including the prosecutors and other law enforcement officials, who made this happen.

I Spent 30 Years There One Morning

The FBI brought all of us together for a presentation followed by a question-and-answer session the night before Danny Heinrich's sentencing. We met in a conference room at the hotel where we stayed. Not all the Paynesville victims came to the sentencing for various reasons. The victim advocate, the supervisory agent, and the special agent who solved the case were there. In the presentation, they described how they caught Heinrich and answered questions. As each victim was pictured in the presentation, we saw the younger versions of ourselves, and the memories came flooding back. We listened, asked questions, and reminisced, finally thanking the FBI for their diligence, attention to us, and for including us. Some of us hadn't seen each other for decades, yet the common bond of fighting Chester had remained strong. The next day, we would be in the long-awaited courtroom.

On a cold, windy November 21, 2016, in downtown Minneapolis, with wind whipping around the buildings just before Thanksgiving, Danny Heinrich faced a public accounting of some of his crimes. He had been free until 2015. Surrounded by news media, we waited in the foyer of the Federal Courthouse until our names were cross-referenced with the security clearance list. Boeckers was there, along with Lauren Schmitz. Jared's family members and some of the Paynesville victims and their wives were there too, waiting. We had all waited. And waited. This day was thirty years in the making for the Paynesville victims. Passing through TSA-like security and up the elevators, we went to a side room where we waited a little longer before entering the courtroom. The FBI representatives were there with us, asking if we had any questions and going over the protocol, explaining how things would proceed. Like a funeral procession, court staff and security ushered us to the courtroom door where we waited again. Standing strategically next to Kirk, I wanted to ensure I could sit by him in court. After everything we had been through together, all the years of waiting, I couldn't miss the chance to sit with him. It was unbelievable. We were about to see the man in the light who had stalked us from the shadows. The man we knew only as "Chester" was going to prison, finally.

Seated together, our sweaty hands clasped—now in our for-ties—two dear childhood friends on either side of me, including Kirk, who had been attacked twice, the Paynesville victims waited. In a courtroom experience that was nothing short of sur-real to me, rivaling any television depiction of suspense, three of us held hands in solidarity and strength. This wasn't TV. We had wondered and waited for a day like this for almost 30 years, never imagining there was even a chance it would happen. Thanks to Jared Scheierl, the Wetterlings, and the Paynesville survivors, this was a day of reckoning, and no one could ignore the connections any longer. Aaron Larson, Trevor Wetterling, and his sisters, Amy and Carmen, were there. My heart went out to them. Aaron had lost his friend, and the Wetterlings had lost their brother; today, the man who took his life was in their midst and would face an accounting.

My heart raced, not unlike the night I sprinted to my apart-ment to call the police on him so long ago; it all came back as we sat, waiting. This was the first time we had seen him in the light. Fat and walking with a limp, he was a pitiful fraction of the physical condition he had been in when I saw him sprint across the church parking lot so long ago, and so frequently in my mind for decades. A slight, fleeting twinge of silent protest stirred inside me when the judge referred to him as "Mr. Hein-rich." "No," I thought, "that's Chester the Molester." A feeling of incongruence—that he did not deserve that respect—rose into my throat, and at the same time, a sensation akin to pity was present as well. Emotions welled up from inside me that I can scarcely name, but gratefully, anger, rage, hatred, and resent-ment didn't make the list. I knew and had lived through some of the abject hell he had caused for so many people. That he took part of Jared and took Jacob's life made me want to scream. Over 30 years after the hell he put us through in Paynesville, and being the boogeyman for so long afterward, wreaking psychological havoc on so many people's lives, he stood there, powerless over his fate, the way he had made his victims feel powerless so long before. Wondering what he might have experienced in his own life, attempting to understand, I tried to tell myself he was a victim, that he was sick. This never made my feelings go away, or even dissipate much, but it served to rationalize how a person could end up the way Danny Heinrich did. I recalled the mind games, the running up the stairs, the counting, timing, and all the requisite survival techniques. I thought of the faith I tried to maintain to get me through, helping me survive. I thought of all the friendships I had developed over the years, the people in Paynesville who took care of me while I was going through it. We sat and listened to the attorneys, both prosecutors and defense. We heard some victims' statements—powerful and moving.

I cried, along with almost everyone in the courtroom, as Jared Scheierl and Aaron Larson, Trevor, Carmen, and Amy Wetterling gave their statements. Etched in my memory is Carmen Wetterling—reading her statement through tears and grief. The Wetterlings shared their sorrowful accounts of the effects Heinrich's actions had on them, their words piercing my heart with deep sadness and pain. Jerry Wetterling thanked Heinrich for letting the family finally know what happened to their son. Heinrich spoke. Most people probably ignored his apologetic-sounding words. Jared, unable to listen, walked out of the courtroom. The judge gave the Paynesville victims a chance to write statements, too. Many of us did, and these were included in the court records.

Matter-of-factly, the judge went over the arrangements the legal teams had come up with, including the sentence. The judge expressed a tone of disbelief over what Heinrich did to Jacob, Jared, and us. He pointed out that while the court documents stated a one-count charge of child pornography the court had levied against Heinrich, the case was really about Jacob, Jared, and the other victims. The judge reviewed the details, making it clear that he believed when Heinrich's sentence ended, officials would assess him for civil commitment and that he would not likely be free. Of course, I pray Danny Heinrich never walks another moment as a free man. When the sentencing ended, people dispersed. It felt like leaving a lecture as we filed out. I remember thinking to myself, "That's it?" My reaction wasn't negative, just anticlimactic. We headed downstairs and Kirk and I waited for Jared. Reporters waited around for us, asking for statements and comments; they knew who we were. Jared spoke to reporters outside the courthouse. Just as we had walked in, we walked out—survivors in our own right. Having always been on the fringe of the investigation for nearly 30 years, we knew we mattered to this case. To commemorate the day's events in a peaceful, somber, low-key manner, we went out to a late lunch, enjoying the long-awaited victory, of sorts.

A Stop in Paynesville

Leaving the restaurant in Minneapolis and heading west, I took Highway 55 toward Paynesville. I thought about all we had been through, all we had seen, and kept thinking about how, after thirty years, these felt like passing moments. Alone and reminiscing, I recalled riding the school bus to and from the Metrodome in Minneapolis as a kid going on field trips to see the Minnesota Twins.

In a symbolic gesture, I knew I had to return to the river, perhaps to reclaim the territory from Heinrich, to reclaim the part of myself that Heinrich took from me so long ago.

I had to show Jared where Heinrich had come from as he ran out from behind the spruce trees. I doubt I had been back since the night Heinrich lurked behind the tree by our campsite. After that night, out of pure necessity and safety, I had to deem the area unsafe and off-limits. The beloved river, once such a sanctuary, my last bastion, was now tarnished and destroyed. Almost 30 years later, with Heinrich in custody and spending real time with Jared, I had to show him the places where the attacks went down. Jared had to be there with me, where Heinrich had run from behind the spruces that May night in 1987. I had to show him our spot on the river, the river that passes, bubbling and talking right behind his house, on the property Jared bought from his dad; the property his dad had inherited and moved to Paynesville, when he had moved to start fresh, to protect his little boy from Danny Heinrich.

Now grown men with our own children, we went down to the riverbank by the trestle with the same enthusiasm as the intrepid, youthful versions of ourselves. Unlike the changes in us, not much had changed in the landscape. We walked down less recklessly than we would have years before. As we walked around the river bottom, I showed Jared where Heinrich had laid for us in wait when we were camping. Jared had been living in

Paynesville for over 25 years by that point. This day, our journey had come full circle.

Files Released: 2018

Paraphrasing, there's an old adage that a story has three sides: my side, your side, and the truth, which is usually somewhere in the middle. The Stearns County Sheriff's Office released most of the case files, allowing the public access to documents pertaining to the case. For almost 30 years, I'd wondered who Chester was. For the most part, I had given up hope of bringing Chester to justice. Decades passed with law enforcement on the brink of apprehending Danny Heinrich. As a suspect in Jacob Wetterling's abduction, he had been interviewed and followed, yet he remained free for decades. Finally, due to Jared's tenacity, a new cold case review, and a DNA match, it happened—Heinrich was the man. Law enforcement finally solved the case.

The FBI got thousands of documents back into its possession, but Stearns County released files from Jared's and Jacob's cases in September of 2018. John Sanner's replacement as interim sheriff was Don Gudmundson, a former Detroit homicide detective who also held other positions in law enforcement agencies, including that of police chief in another Minnesota municipality. He managed the release of the Stearns County documents and held a press conference on the day of the release. Sheriff Gudmundson mentioned the tip I provided within 48 hours of Jacob's abduction during the press conference.[17] I appreciated this and looked forward to the opportunity to review the documents myself one day. As I've mentioned, the documents are voluminous. Reading through them informed my views of the cases with a much wider lens and changed some of my previously held perceptions.

---

[17] WCCO Television. "Stearns Co. Sheriff Blasts Early Stage of Wetterling Investigation." September 20, 2018 at 4:10 pm. https://minnesota.cbslocal.com/2018/09/20/sheriff-admits-wetterling-investigation-botched/

PART V
PURPOSE

CHAPTER 11
Traumanomics

There is a psychic cost children bear
when they grow up in fear. ~John Niven

This story doesn't end with Danny Heinrich heading to prison. Having read my book, or having read about the cases elsewhere, empathy probably comes easily for most people. It's likely easy, too, to question the investigation and perhaps cheer on the people who brought it all together. An incredible undertaking and effort by many people and officials finally closed the case. The case started monumental changes in policing, parenting, mental health and counseling, education, and other areas. People took an interest in these cases, and seeing the outcome: good had finally triumphed over evil. I believe that is true. I also believe more good came from the entire situation than one could have ever predicted, including, for example, people's decades of advocacy, like Patty Wetterling's. In cases like these, remaining unsolved for so long, I would guess that observers, most likely and understandably, bookend their knowledge—at least those old enough to remember the events, that is. Consider someone in their 20s in 1989, for example. They remember hearing about Jacob's abduction, the initial investigation, the investigation stalling, and time passing; decades pass while he or she lives out his or her life. Imagine, for example, a couple finishing college, falling in love, getting married, having children, and possibly grandchildren before law enforcement solved the case. To those who were not directly involved, it probably faded away. Not for us.

Most people probably heard about various bits and pieces of the investigation over the years until one day, in 2015, officials came up with the right evidence to solve the case, at which time observers shared in the satisfaction of the resolution, perhaps recalling how they originally heard about it, thereby creating the bookends.

A lot went on during those years, both in the investigation and in people's lives. Like any life experiences, traumatic or not, time moved on, leaving effects behind. When law enforcement reopened the case—although it was never technically closed—and solved it, I was (and am) grateful to have seen all the love and support poured out for those involved, including that from communities, media, and individuals, as well as from many in law enforcement.

Prevention and Help

I believe the work is just beginning. It's a great time to acknowledge and continue to underscore the personal and economic effects of crime and trauma on our communities, states, and the nation. To make meaningful change, it has to be safe for people to tell their stories and for us to provide support and resources for healing. I think this is especially true for boys. At the time of Heinrich's attacks, most of us knew nothing about any resources available for counseling, assistance, and the like. This has changed, and the stigma of telling the story is less than it used to be, but there's still a very long way to go. Obviously, most traumatic experiences don't have the media attention these cases received, but it's incumbent upon all of us to do our part to help others and to break the cycles that perpetuate violence and abuse. What are the stakes?

With a very rough estimate, I mentioned that Heinrich affected the victims with an aggregate of 400 years of experience. I say "experience," as opposed to "abuse," "turmoil," or some other word, because there has been much good that has come out of these experiences for people. There has also been much PTSD, addiction, relationship strife, trauma of all types including financial loss, abuse, and so on. I think this is the purpose for telling stories and seeking help. Cases like this can be a wake-up call to society and a call to action to change how we handle situations and to break the old rules, like messages to boys of "Be a man" and "Toughen up." I want to imagine many cases like ours society can avoid by asking questions and assisting children so they don't grow up and continue to perpetuate the violence and abuse they've experienced.

Economics

This is not an academic book, but my own educational experiences in undergrad and three advanced degrees permeate my thinking and vision. In addition to the extensive personal, emotional, familial, and societal impacts of this case and ones like it, there is a plethora of economic outcomes to consider, too. Speaking in economic terms, there is an opportunity cost to the experiences we had—that is, we lost something of value. The true definition of opportunity cost is that we lost something because we chose something else. It could be like losing the opportunity to have a cookie because I chose a brownie instead.

With trauma, people do not choose it, but there can be tremendous costs. A discussion about this would be another book. People have studied and written about this, but my point is that I have experienced and seen people struggle economically and financially because of their traumatic experiences. These traumas manifest in a range from not doing well at work, to not working at all, to not being able to thrive in economic pursuits—to name a few. Economic problems can perpetuate further trauma, and the cycle continues. On the other hand, many people who experience unbelievable traumatic events succeed despite their circumstances. My hope is that we can create supportive environments and systems for people in all walks of life to be their best.

Closing Remarks

In one of the rarest types of crimes statistically, there were multiple unnerving similarities and connections within a 30-mile area in central Minnesota, but officials did not have the right pieces to convict the perpetrator. With Jared Scheierl's tenacity and fresh look, officials obtained the DNA evidence needed to solve the case. I have camped in the pasture where Danny Heinrich buried Jacob Wetterling. Having wondered about it for decades, I was not surprised when he led authorities there. I had such an initial feeling of hope and elation when law enforcement arrested a suspect and was in disbelief in 1990 when law enforcement did not solve the cases with a connection to Paynesville.

I know there are a wide range of experiences and a wide variety of stories—in fact, for every human, there's a story. Some people have it worse than others, and it's relative. While I don't know what drove Danny Heinrich to commit these crimes, there is a story. Start talking about your experience; there are resources and people available to help you get through things. Fear can have the power to keep us stuck, but fear can be replaced by courage. For me, faith and friendship rose to the top when I needed help the most.

I learned a great deal through my own therapy sessions and have since continued my education in the mental health field. I'm a teacher by training and at heart. I have been around many people in various settings and work with all sorts of them. When people go through difficult situations and traumatic events, there are lasting effects that are likely to surface, and often—I dare say, usually—cause trouble. I've experienced these effects. Friends or family members likely come to mind as you think of the people you know who struggle in some way or another. Many clinicians and academics study PTSD. My experiences have left me with a number of issues I've worked to put behind me or utilize whenever possible, such as the fear that Heinrich caused.

For many years, decades, I felt voiceless. I felt voiceless in my efforts to bring attention to the Paynesville attacks; all the Paynesville survivors must have felt voiceless on some level—but they matter. I've used this book to share some perspectives on the experiences I had with Heinrich, Jared, and Jacob. Knowing all too well what it's like to feel powerless, hopeless, and filled with despair, I'm using these last few pages to share what I believe may be helpful to the voiceless going forward.

I believe we've only begun to crack the door open a little more than the #MeToo movement opened it previously. There is so much more work to do in breaking down the walls that prevent boys, girls, men, and women from sharing their stories and beginning the healing process. Until this happens, the pain and effects of trauma will continue to affect generations. I believe this story is one of resilience. I think it can be a source of hope for people who are going through traumatic experiences, such as abuse at home or elsewhere. I pray that they (you) will come to know that they (you) can survive and thrive.

Personally, reconciling the fact that the child who went through the experiences in Paynesville turned out to be the same man who is now a reasonably successful, productive adult has been a struggle. It's as though there were two lives going on next to each other; I've always felt as if they weren't the same person. Difficult to explain, it's a feeling like being an impostor, counterfeit, or a fraud. It's almost as if there were two different people growing up juxtaposed with one another, and the adult version can peer into the life of the younger.

I'm not sure why I possess this scrappiness and a desire to fight and survive. There have been times in my life when the desire has waxed and waned, but I've never given up. I've always believed it's important to try, even when I fail. Even in some of the darkest times of my life, in the pit of despair, lacking much hope, during active alcoholism as well as sobriety, I have always found a way to persevere, somehow, for some reason.

I made it by relying upon friends, coworkers, prayer, meditation, exercise, podcasts, YouTube videos, books, and whatever else was required of me; I've tried everything. It has been years of struggle, fighting the message, "You don't matter," but the reality is that we do matter—all people matter. All people have gifts, talents, and much to contribute, with vast potential. You survivors matter, and despite the most incredible trauma, you can be resilient and work through things to better yourself. You deserve to become the best version of yourself possible and, most importantly, to be of service and an example to others. You don't have to go down (or stay on) a path of substance abuse, process addiction, unhealthy relationships, or continue living in unsafe conditions, nor repeat the pattern of abuse you may be in or are working through presently. You don't have to resign yourself to an unfulfilling life. You deserve to have joy, and it can happen. You can grow, live well, and you can be better. Don't accept less than your full potential.

Researchers from various academic disciplines are exploring relationships between trauma, the brain, and characteristics such as grit and perseverance. For parents, mental health and medical professionals, law enforcement officials, and those in the helping professions, this is a call to action—a call to serve others and provide hope to those who suffer alone. All people have a journey, and each journey includes pain, joy, obstacles, and relative hardships; and I believe all people can be helpful to others in some measure. Sharing one's experiences, stories, and effects, and showing resilience, can be a great symbol of hope. Being available and making oneself vulnerable opens a door to being helpful to others. If I reach and am helpful to at least one other person, I will claim success with this book.

My hope is that our stories may be symbols of hope for the many children and adults, young and old, who are struggling to feel safe, to share their stories, and to heal from their respective traumatic experiences. I persevered; I kept on, made it, and thrived. In addition to an insider's view of a tragic story, my hope for you is that you gain a general understanding of the experiences of trauma victims—they vary widely, of course. I hope people will pause and reflect on the reasons for the behaviors they see in students and perhaps their own children, and not be afraid to ask questions. Simply asking, "Are you OK?" can go a long way and open doors to hope and healing. One of the most meaningful compliments I receive from time to time is when I share my experiences and people say they would have never expected me to have such a background and experience. We have a responsibility to provide safe environments for children, to listen to their stories, affirm and validate their experiences, and work to create a world where kids can ride their bikes.

BIBLIOGRAPHY

Douglass, Tim. "Charged with Molesting Boys, Belgrade Man Arrested." *Paynesville Press*, January 1, 1990.

Haukebo, Kirsten. "Two abductions may be linked." *St. Cloud Times,* December 14, 1989. https://www.newspapers.com/article/st-cloud-times/136435741/

Raguse, Lou. "Heinrich as Suspect: A Timeline." Last modified September 14, 2016. https://www.kare11.com/article/news/crime/heinrich-as-suspect-a-timeline/314467341

Stearns County Sheriff's Office, "Case # 89006407 Wetterling Homicide case files." St. Cloud, MN 2018.

Thyen, Darlene. "Local Police Seek Help in Accosting Incidences." *Paynesville Press*, May 26, 1987.

Thyen, Darlene. "Police Still Working for Arrest." *Paynesville Press*, June 23, 1987.

Unze, David. "DNA Cracked Wetterling Case." *The St. Cloud Times,* September 23, 2016. https://www.sctimes.com/story/news/local/2016/09/23/dna-cracked-wetterling-case/90849308/

Van der Kolk, Bessel, A. *The Body Keeps the Score: Brain, Mind, and Body in the Healing of Trauma.* New York: Viking, 2014.

WCCO Television. "Stearns Co. Sheriff Blasts Early Stage of Wetterling Investigation." September 20, 2018, at 4:10 pm. https://minnesota.cbslocal.com/2018/09/20/sheriff-admits-wetterling-investigation-botched/

Cold Spring Record Article. Cold Spring Record, "Crime Stoppers Needs Public's Information," (Cold Spring, MN), Feb. 7, 1989

TESTIMONIAL

The waves of pain and trauma caused by personal crimes cascade through families and friends, and communities. The toil and costs are too often hidden, unrecognized and repeated. Kris Bertelsen's courageous sharing of his personal journey offers a firsthand account of his experiences and observations in the aftermath of devasting crimes and the limitations of our societal institutions to offer answers and needed assistance even when individuals in those institutions are so often caring and dedicated professionals. During the time span recounted during "Pain in Paynesville," I've witnessed firsthand a growing recognition and expanding emphasis on improving communications and services to those impacted by crimes. We are hopefully getting better—but still have such a long way to go. Dr. Bertelsen's insights and experiences offer opportunities for reflection and discussion as we all try to close that distance from where we were to where we would hope to be.

~Chris Boeckers, Federal Law Enforcement Agent, Retired

ACKNOWLEDGMENT

I would like to express my sincere gratitude to so many people for their support, not only as I wrote this book, but from many people, for decades of friendship, and in some cases, providing safety.

I want to thank those Paynesville community members who supported us as we dealt with the unspeakable in the mid-1980s. Thank you to the friends who went through the terror in Paynesville. Your experiences matter. Thank you to those friends and family who supported us in those times of tremendous fear and years beyond. Thank you to law enforcement agencies and officers, particularly Sargent Bill Drager, who showed his concern and worked diligently to protect children in Paynesville, and to law enforcement officials who never stopped trying to solve the cases. Thank you to Jerry Wetterling for meeting with me in 1989, and to him and Patty for their example of strength over the years. Thank you to the federal prosecutors and Stearns County Attorney Janelle Kendall for their efforts and explanations.

I'd like to express my gratitude to Chris Boeckers, who walked us through the entire process from when the case started receiving renewed interest, to the day Danny Heinrich was sentenced. Thank you to Lauren Schmitz for her advocacy and support for victims. I want to thank the following members of media; Mike Jacobson, Deborah Roberts, Karla Hult, Esme Murphy, and Dan Austreng.

I became overwhelmed with appreciation as I considered the list of people deserving acknowledgment in this book. In some instances, I did not name people to protect their anonymity. I'm relying on the fact that you know who you are; thank you my friends.

RESOURCES

Upstart Resilience www.Upstartresilience.com

National Alliance on Mental Illness www.nami.org

National Institute of Mental Health

https://www.nimh.nih.gov/

Substance Abuse and Mental Health Services

Administration

https://www.samhsa.gov/

www.ingramcontent.com/pod-product-compliance
Lightning Source LLC
Chambersburg PA
CBHW060225030426
42335CB00014B/1342